KNIGHT-CAPRON LIBRARY
LYNCHBURG COLLEGE
LYNCHBURG, VIRGINIA 24501

WITHDRAWN

Hugh MacLennan

Twayne's World Authors Series
Canadian Literature

Robert Lecker, Editor
McGill University

TWAS 708

HUGH MACLENNAN
(1907–   )
Photograph courtesy of Peter Paterson

Hugh MacLennan

By T. D. MacLulich

Twayne Publishers • *Boston*

KNIGHT-CAPRON LIBRARY
LYNCHBURG COLLEGE
LYNCHBURG, VIRGINIA 24501

PR
9199
.3
.M334
Z69
1983

Hugh MacLennan

T. D. MacLulich

Copyright © 1983 by G.K. Hall & Company
All Rights Reserved
Published by Twayne Publishers
A Division of G. K. Hall & Company
70 Lincoln Street
Boston, Massachusetts 02111

Book Production by Marne B. Sultz

Book Design by Barbara Anderson

Printed on permanent/durable acid-free paper and bound in the United States of America.

Library of Congress Cataloging in Publication Data

MacLulich, T. D. (Thomas Donald), 1943–
Hugh MacLennan.

(Twayne's world authors series ; TWAS 708)
Bibliography: p. 135
Includes index.
1. MacLennan, Hugh, 1907–
Criticism and interpretation.
I. Title. II. Series.
PR9199.3.M334Z69 1983 813'.54 83-10667
ISBN 0-8057-6555-7

For My Parents

Contents

About the Author
Preface
Acknowledgments
Chronology

> *Chapter One*
> Father and Son   1
>
> *Chapter Two*
> Young Men of 1933   17
>
> *Chapter Three*
> National Romances   31
>
> *Chapter Four*
> The Calvinist Legacy   53
>
> *Chapter Five*
> Requiem and Renewal   78
>
> *Chapter Six*
> Psychology and History   94
>
> *Chapter Seven*
> Man of Letters   118

Notes and References   129
Selected Bibliography   135
Index   140

About the Author

T. D. MacLulich did graduate work in Canadian literature at Simon Fraser University and at York University. He has published articles on many aspects of Canadian writing and has taught at the Universities of Alberta, Lethbridge, Manitoba, and Victoria.

Preface

For a brief period during the late 1960s, Hugh MacLennan was very much excited by a proposal made by the film producer Lester Cowan to turn the novel *Two Solitudes* into a movie. At one point the suggestion was made to him that the anticlimax in the second half of *Two Solitudes* might be circumvented by combining *Two Solitudes* and the recently published *Return of the Sphinx* into a single film. Although *Return of the Sphinx* is ostensibly a sequel to another of MacLennan's novels, *Each Man's Son*, MacLennan readily agreed with the suggestion. He saw the combined story as a cinematic epic telling the story of Canada during the twentieth century, much as the film of *Doctor Zhivago* tells Russia's story. The two novels could easily be combined, MacLennan suggested, if Alan Ainslie's name were changed to Paul Tallard. He added, "Essentially, Ainslie and Tallard are very similar characters, being as it were projections of some very basic aspects of myself."[1]

The film was never made;[2] but the incident illustrates several lessons I have tried to keep in mind while writing this study. MacLennan appears here in a role he has frequently adopted, that of a self-appointed spokesman for Canadian society. Indeed, MacLennan's novels are often interpreted as a set of variations on the theme of Canadian national identity. But this view of MacLennan is a partial one. Certainly, there is a considerable degree of unity among his novels, which makes it possible to see them as successive chapters in a single extended work. However, as MacLennan's comment on Ainslie and Tallard suggests, the most persistent themes of his fiction are personal rather than national. His protagonists have aged at the same rate he has and have been assigned many incidents and character traits borrowed from his own life. His novels closely follow his development from youthful discontent to the reflective calm of old age.

My study argues that MacLennan's writing was shaped as much by private emotional imperatives as by reasoned responses to external political and social conditions. MacLennan has sought to exorcise his personal demons at the same time as he has searched for a satisfactory accommodation between the individual and the modern world. Read in chronological order, his novels and essays record the emotional, intellectual, and spiritual odyssey on which he has been embarked throughout his adult life. At this point I should enter a disclaimer. I am not writing a full-scale biography of MacLennan. That task has recently been accomplished, with commendable thoroughness, by Elspeth Cameron. Indeed, I have shamelessly raided Cameron's book for information about the facts of MacLennan's life. Insofar as my book is biographical, it traces an inner development, both emotional and intellectual, which is publicly revealed through the symbolic actions depicted in MacLennan's novels.

The narrator of Dostoyevsky's *Notes from Underground* asserts that there are "some things that a man is afraid to reveal even to himself, and any honest man accumulates a pretty fair number of such things." As a result, Dostoyevsky's narrator endorses Heine's statement "that trustworthy autobiographies are almost an impossibility, and that a man will probably never tell the truth about himself."[3] It may happen, then, that autobiography is most true when it takes the form of fiction, for in the guise of fiction an author may unknowingly confess those things he is afraid to tell even to himself. Some such process, I will contend, has occurred in MacLennan's novels.

T. D. MacLulich

Acknowledgments

Several passages in this study derive from my article "Oedipus and Eve: The Novels of Hugh MacLennan," *Dalhousie Review* 59 (Autumn 1979):500–518. My discussion of *The Precipice* is based on *"The Precipice:* MacLennan's Anatomy of Failure," *Journal of Canadian Studies* 14 (Winter 1979–80):54–65. Chapter 5 includes a short section taken from "Colloquial Style and the Tory Mode," *Canadian Literature,* no. 89 (Summer 1981), pp. 7–21. I am grateful to the editors of *Dalhousie Review, Journal of Canadian Studies,* and *Canadian Literature* for permission to make use of this material. The quotations from Hugh MacLennan's letters and unpublished novels appear by permission of Hugh MacLennan. The passage from Margaret Laurence's letter to Hugh MacLennan appears by permission of Margaret Laurence. Research for this study was aided by a grant from the University of Victoria, using funds provided by the Social Sciences and Humanities Research Council of Canada. Lawrence Mathews read the entire manuscript and offered many useful suggestions.

Chronology

1907	John Hugh MacLennan born 20 March to Dr. Samuel MacLennan and Katherine MacQuarrie MacLennan, in Glace Bay, Nova Scotia.
1913	Dr. MacLennan studied in Edinburgh, Vienna, and Berlin. His family joined him in London for the summer.
1913–1914	Dr. MacLennan completed his specialist's degree (ear, nose, and throat) at Columbia University.
1914–1915	The MacLennan family lived in Sydney, Nova Scotia.
1915	In September the family moved to Halifax, Nova Scotia. Dr. MacLennan enlisted in the Canadian Army and went overseas.
1916	Dr. MacLennan invalided home in December.
1917	Halifax Explosion occurred on 6 December.
1924–1928	MacLennan attended Dalhousie Univeristy in Halifax. In graduation year, won Governor-General's Gold Medal in Classics. Awarded Rhodes Scholarship for Canada-at-large.
1927	Won Nova Scotia doubles tennis championship.
1928–1932	Studied "Mods and Greats" at Oriel College, Oxford. Played rugger for his college and tennis for the university. Spent vacations traveling on the continent.
1929	Won Maritimes singles tennis championship while home during summer vacation.
1932	Received Oxford B.A. with second class in "Mods" and third class in "Greats." Applied for a job in the classics department at Dalhousie, but was refused in favor of an Englishman.
1932–1935	Doctoral candidate in classics at Princeton University. Spent summers touring the northern states. Began to write fiction.

1933	A novel, "So All Their Praises," was accepted by a firm that went bankrupt before publishing the book.
1935	Awarded Ph.D. for his thesis *Oxyrhynchus: An Economic and Social Study*.
1935–1945	Taught history and classics at Lower Canada College in Montreal.
1936	Married Dorothy Duncan.
1937	Completed a novel, "A Man Should Rejoice." Several publishers showed interest, but all eventually declined the book. Toured Russia in the summer.
1939	MacLennan's father died.
1941	*Barometer Rising*.
1943–1944	Awarded Guggenheim Fellowship to work on a novel. Spent winter in New York.
1945	*Two Solitudes*. Given Governor-General's Award for fiction. Resigned from Lower Canada College.
1948	*The Precipice*. Given Governor-General's Award for fiction.
1949	*Cross-Country*. Given Governor-General's Award for nonfiction.
1951	*Each Man's Son*. Began part-time teaching at McGill University in Montreal.
1952	Elected Fellow of the Royal Society of Canada; given the Lorne Pierce Medal for Literature by the society.
1954	*Thirty and Three*. Given Governor-General's Award for nonfiction.
1956	Made a Fellow of the Royal Society of Literature.
1957	Dorothy Duncan died.
1959	*The Watch That Ends the Night*. Given Governor-General's Award for fiction. Married Frances Aline Walker of Montreal.
1960	*Scotchman's Return and Other Essays*.
1961	*Seven Rivers of Canada*.
1963–1964	Awarded special Canada Council grant. Spent winter in France working on a novel.

Chronology

1966   Received Molson Award.
1967   *Return of the Sphinx.* Received Royal Bank Award, and was made Companion of the Order of Canada.
1968   Promoted to full professor at McGill.
1974   *Rivers of Canada.*
1978   *The Other Side of Hugh MacLennan.*
1979   Retired from McGill; made professor emeritus and continued to teach one course.
1980   *Voices in Time.*

Chapter One
Father and Son

Hugh MacLennan is Canada's leading literary nationalist. More directly than any other Canadian writer, he creates characters who inhabit a specifically Canadian society and whose fates are linked to the political fortunes of the nation. Yet MacLennan was for a long time a reluctant nationalist. His two early unpublished novels dealt with "international" themes. He used a Canadian setting in *Barometer Rising* only grudgingly, after he had reluctantly concluded that a perverse fate had doomed him to be a "Canadian" writer. Then in *Two Solitudes* he somewhat opportunistically mined the vein of Canadian approval he had struck with the publication of *Barometer Rising*.

For many readers in the 1940s, *Barometer Rising* and *Two Solitudes* seemed to fill a vacuum in Canadian letters. The books were welcomed for their Canadian subject matter and their nationalist themes; their artistic flaws were readily forgiven. Nonetheless, in writing his third novel, which is set partly in the United States, MacLennan deliberately tried to break through to the larger American market; he desperately wanted to write a best-seller. Only when *The Precipice* met a lukewarm reception did he fully resign himself to writing from his native background, and throughout his career he has continued to seek an international readership.

MacLennan's emphasis on explicitly political themes sets him apart from most other Canadian novelists. But in many other ways his work shows similarities to the work of other writers of his generation. Like Sinclair Ross, Ernest Buckler, W. O. Mitchell, and later Margaret Laurence, MacLennan depicts characters who resist the inertia and restrictiveness of a philistine society and who labor under the inhibitions left by a puritanical family background. Like many members of his literary generation, MacLennan takes as a central theme in his work the hostility shown to the sensitive individual by society, and he shows the great price the individual pays for following a private vision rather than conforming to the community's expectations.

In addition to his novels, MacLennan has published a great amount of nonfiction. Some of his personal essays possess an enduring charm, but his more ambitious attempts at social and political analysis have not worn well. MacLennan is not a systematic thinker; his conservative perspective on politics, education, and literature is emotionally rather than intellectually motivated. Moreover, his nonfiction is often part of a strategic ground-clearing operation, a preparation for the writing of his next novel. His discussions of politics and society are frequently reflections of private concerns, and his literary theories are usually defenses of his own kind of art.

MacLennan's reputation will continue to rest primarily on the best of his novels. *Barometer Rising* and *Two Solitudes* have earned a permanent place in Canadian literary history. Artistically, they are qualified successes, but by virtue of their pioneering depiction of characters who are integral parts of the Canadian milieu, they will continue to be read and studied. Two later novels, *Each Man's Son* and *The Watch That Ends the Night,* represent the peak of MacLennan's achievement. *Each Man's Son* is a powerful study of the Calvinist ethos that informs the work of so many Canadian authors; and *The Watch That Ends the Night* is MacLennan's most mature and self-confident fictional statement, his most eloquent affirmation of the significance of human life. MacLennan's other novels—*The Precipice, Return of the Sphinx,* and *Voices in Time*—are marred by excessive didacticism and by superficial characterizations; they are too obviously lessons presented in fictional form.

Although the quality of MacLennan's work is uneven, his career nonetheless exhibits an unmistakable unity. Indeed, taken as a whole, MacLennan's writings constitute a revealing record of his intellectual and emotional development. The more public or political dimensions of MacLennan's literary career are relatively well-known. The private significance of his writings is less familiar to most readers. To understand the personal meaning of MacLennan's work, the reader requires some knowledge of MacLennan's life. Much of the necessary information has been provided by MacLennan himself in the autobiographical passages contained in many of his essays. In these personal asides, he offers some vivid vignettes of the Cape Breton and the Halifax of his boyhood; and he reveals the biographical basis for a theme that is at the very heart of his fiction—the divided feelings of a dutiful but independent-minded son toward a demanding and undemonstrative father.

The Reluctant Canadian

Hugh MacLennan was born in the Cape Breton mining town of Glace Bay in 1907, "during a blizzard that shook my father's house as a north easterly gale drove the Atlantic thundering against the rocky shores of Cape Breton Island."[1] Although his father's family had lived in Cape Breton for three generations, they still thought of themselves as "Scotch" and kept alive the memory of the land they had been forced to leave during the infamous Highland clearances, when sheep displaced tenant farmers in many Highland glens. As a legacy from his Highland ancestors, MacLennan acquired a habit of moody introspection, a sense of belonging to a wronged people, and a conception of human nature that was deeply rooted in Calvinist theology. His upbringing created an outlook that was strongly ethnic, sectarian, and regional, so that he later described himself as "a Scotsman, a Presbyterian and a Nova Scotian."[2] MacLennan's sense of Canadian identity was acquired later in life, and he may have brought some of the zeal of the convert to his new faith.

MacLennan's parents were temperamental opposites; his father was self-disciplined and slow to show emotion, whereas his mother was outgoing and vivacious. The persistence of MacLennan's feeling for his mother is indicated by his subsequent attraction to women who resembled her and by his portrayal of such women in his fiction.[3] But it was his father, "Dr. Sam" MacLennan, who exerted the more obvious shaping influence on MacLennan's development. Dr. Sam was a stern and demanding parent, and a formidable exponent of the Calvinist view that man was put on earth to do his duty to God, not to enjoy himself. In MacLennan's home, as in all the Presbyterian households with which he was familiar, "the Sabbath was kept holy by a ban on pleasures of every kind."[4] Of his father, MacLennan has written:

He was entirely Scotch; he was a living specimen of a most curious heritage. In spite of his medical knowledge, which was large; in spite of his quick nervous vitality and tireless energy, he was never able to lay to rest the beasties which went bump in his mind at three o'clock in the morning. It mattered nothing that he was a third-generation Canadian who had never seen the Highlands before he visited them on leave in the First World War. He never needed to go there to understand whence he came or what he was. He was neither a Scot nor yet was he Scottish; he never used those genteel appellations which are now supposed to be *de rigueur*. He was simply Scotch. All the perplexity and doggedness of the race was in him, its loneliness, tenderness and affection, its deceptive vitality, its quick flashes of violence, its dog-whistle sensitivity to sounds to which Anglo-Saxons are stone-deaf, its incapacity to tell its heart to foreigners save in terms foreigners do not comprehend, its resigned indifference to whether they comprehend or not. "It's not easy being Scotch," he told me more than once. To which I suppose another Scotchman might say: "It wasn't meant to be."[5]

Dr. Sam presented a reserved facade to the world, he imposed high standards on himself and on others, and he imbued his son with his own Calvinist sense of imminent and inescapable doom. MacLennan admired his father's skill, knowledge, and self-control. He wished to earn approval by emulating his father's apparent self-assurance. But Dr. Sam's self-discipline had another side: he was restraining something within himself. For example, MacLennan reports, "My father never touched liquor; he admitted frankly that he was afraid of it, and I suppose this was another way of saying that he was afraid of himself."[6] Certainly such a man could be difficult to live with and might inspire fear as well as admiration.

Although MacLennan left Cape Breton at eight years of age, the island and its people made their mark on him. One of his best novels, *Each Man's Son,* is set in a town resembling Glace Bay, and the novel's protagonist, Dr. Daniel Ainslie, acts as physician to a community of miners, as did MacLennan's father. The main industry of Glace Bay was mining, and most of the miners were descendants of the Highland Scots who settled in great numbers in the eastern regions of Nova Scotia. Among these people Gaelic was still a living language, and their English showed the strong Gaelic accent and idiom that MacLennan has reproduced in the dialogue of *Each Man's Son.*

In this community of men he considered little better than barbarians, MacLennan's father was discontented, for his ambition went beyond the patching up of drunken miners. He first put distance between himself and the miners by settling his family "in a small house, encircled by a brook, perched atop a grassy knoll a mile or so inland from the coast."[7] Then in the winter of 1912–13, Dr. Sam used his savings to finance a trip to Europe to study toward a specialist's degree. That spring the entire family followed him to England for several months, and in the fall Dr. Sam went to New York to complete his training. When he returned in January of 1914, the family moved briefly to Sydney, also on Cape Breton. The next year, however, Dr. Sam decided to move to Halifax, which remained MacLennan's home for the next thirteen years.

At that time Halifax was abuzz with wartime activity, which not only excited young Hugh but impinged directly on his life. On Christmas Eve of 1915, he watched his father rise from the supper table, put on his new great coat, and march away at the rear of a column of soldiers. His account of the incident evokes a small boy's bewiderment and unhappiness at seeing his father disappear: "My father fell in behind the last rank and faded off down the half-lit street, holding his head low against the wind to keep his flat military cap from blowing off, and my mother tried to hide her feelings by saying what a shame the cap didn't fit him properly."[8] The departure, which was the culmination of a series of paternal leave-takings, must have been experienced by young Hugh almost as a desertion. These experiences surely contributed to the orphan motif that runs through MacLennan's novels.

MacLennan's father returned shortly before Christmas the next year. MacLennan says his father was "invalided home as a result of excessive work as a surgeon in the hospital," but Cameron reports more prosaically that Dr. Sam was sent home because his arm had become infected.[9] Dr. Sam's first act upon entering the family's newly rented house was to search for the source of a gas smell. He did so, unwisely, by lighting his way down the basement with a match. The results were dramatic. The family experienced "our own private explosion. It smashed the windows in the other houses along the block, it shook the ground like an earthquake and it was heard for a mile."

The headline in the next day's paper was embarrassing to the family: "Doctor Hunts Gas Leak with Burning Match—Finds It!" When MacLennan's father recovered from his injuries, he denied the story. However, young Hugh "had distinctly seen him with the match in his hand, going down to the basement to look for the gas and complaining about how careless people were." MacLennan denies that he lost faith in his father. Instead, he insists, "I wished he had been able to tell his story sooner and stick to it." After all, would patients trust a doctor who had been painted in the newspapers as "an absent-minded veteran looking for a gas leak in a dark basement with a lighted match"? Nonetheless, the incident must have made its mark on young Hugh. The previously infallible father was suddenly shown to be careless and vulnerable.

A year later MacLennan lived through the explosion with which his name has become permanently linked:

One cold, clear December morning, while the boys were playing on the packed ashes about the school, and the first fight of the day was brewing, there was a roar past all hearing, and we saw the windows of the school burst inward and the trees toss, and a teacher stagger out the front door with blood streaming from her face.[10]

Shortly afterwards, he saw "a steady stream of wounded men and women and children, all bloody from horrible glass cuts." Near his own house, "a man was lying in the gutter with his face slit open and his jugular severed and he was already unconscious. The blood was coming out in slow leaps and running easily down a few yards of gutter into the cess-pit on the corner, like water after rain. He had on painter's overalls, and a window had blown right in on his face."[11]

This experience is obviously the major prototype upon which MacLennan draws for his account of the Halifax explosion in *Barometer Rising*. But it seems extremely likely that the earlier, smaller explosion in the family basement also lies behind MacLennan's sense that arbitrary forces often take hold of human lives and rearrange them in apparently random fashion.

At his father's insistence, MacLennan's education stressed the study of classical language and literature. Dr. Sam, himself a constant reader of the classics, set his son the goal of attaining a Rhodes Scholarship. MacLennan never quarreled openly with his overbearing father, but in other ways he did express his resistance to Dr. Sam's influence. For example, from the time he was eleven until his graduation from Dalhousie University, he slept summer and winter in a tent pitched in the family backyard.[12] This unusual regimen surely reflected young Hugh's wish to separate himself from parental influence.

At Dalhousie, MacLennan majored in Greek and Latin, and played basketball on the university team. He also played tennis with sufficient skill to be part of the team that won the men's doubles championship of Nova Scotia in 1927. In his graduating year, MacLennan's combination of athletic and scholastic accomplishments seemed likely to make him a winner of the Rhodes Scholarship Dr. Sam had pointed him toward. But to MacLennan's disappointment, the award for Nova Scotia was given to another Dalhousie student. MacLennan has described how, when news of his own belated award arrived, his father reacted with typically "Scotch" restraint:

I had come home from a walk and discovered, absolutely out of the blue, that a telegram had arrived informing me that I had won a Rhodes Scholarship months after I had believed that I had lost my last chance of getting one. My father had risen to this occasion in the spirit of his ancestors. "Go out and shovel the snow," he said, and it was the only occasion when he ever ordered me to work on the Sabbath Day.[13]

It is no exaggeration to say that, when MacLennan set sail from New York in the late fall of 1928, he went to England and Europe to be civilized. MacLennan had been taught by his father that membership in civilization was not automatic, but had to be earned. This idea persisted throughout MacLennan's life and sometimes found its way into his fiction. For example, in *Return of the Sphinx,* Daniel Ainslie reports that his father "used to talk to me about the necessity of this country *earning* its way into civilization."[14] MacLennan was prepared to regard his Oxford tutors as the embodiment of all that was best in European civilization. Only by earning their approval could he earn approval in his own eyes.

At Oxford, MacLennan read "Mods and Greats," a demanding survey of classical languages, literature, history, and philosophy. But his life during the Oxford years was not all academic drudgery. He played tennis for the university, played rugger for his college, and generally took a full part in college life. His letters home tell of occasional attendance at theaters and concerts; and on one memorable occasion he "sat in the Sheldonian Theatre in Oxford and listened to John Galsworthy read the Romanes Lecture."[15]

On his vacations MacLennan traveled on the continent, visiting Germany, France, Switzerland, Italy, and Greece. These trips were a rewarding combination of work and pleasure. He studied, practiced his languages, and enjoyed meeting an array of people that included one innocuous-looking priest who was later arrested by the Italian authorities as a British spy.[16] While at Oxford, MacLennan also became aware of his ignorance about his native country. Invited to tea with a young British student, MacLennan discovered that the Englishman had toured Canada and knew more about the country than he did.[17]

MacLennan found his Oxford studies very taxing. In his letters, he began to wonder whether high marks were the only criterion by which a student's success could be judged, and he resigned himself to not obtaining the first-class standing he had desired. Occasionally his letters offered mild criticisms of the tutors he had installed in his mind as parental surrogates. But perhaps the closest thing to a direct attack on Dr. Sam is a comment, made about MacLennan's grandfather, that could without change be applied to Dr. Sam himself. "Most of his instincts were kindly and affable," MacLennan wrote in one of his letters home, "but on Sunday, as a sort of religious duty, he sought to make himself unbearable to the whole family."[18]

Perhaps another reason for MacLennan's failure to attain first-class standing was his increasing devotion to the writing of poetry. He attempted at least one long narrative poem, based on a Biblical theme, and in his last year at Oxford, he submitted a volume of shorter poems to a publisher. He claimed in a letter to his sister that the publisher's refusal was based mainly on the poor economic climate rather than on deficiencies in the poems themselves. And he told his sister, only half jokingly: "Indeed, I have a very big grudge at the world. Why? Because the best poet that has appeared since the death of Rupert Brooke and James Elroy Flecker is not being given a chance to put his stuff across."[19]

MacLennan left Oxford in 1932. When he had received his Rhodes Scholarship, his prospects of an academic career had undoubtedly looked bright. However, the Depression had intervened and university posts were now scarce. At first MacLennan thought he would be lucky, for a job opened in his field at his own university, Dalhousie. When he went to see the department head, however, he received the disconcerting news that the job was certain to go to an applicant from England. MacLennan insists that the Englishman's academic qualifications were exactly the same as his own.[20] But, as the professor phrased it, "After all, you're a Canadian and he's an Englishman. It makes a difference."

The rejection by Dalhousie was a crushing experience for MacLennan. He felt unjustly betrayed by the institution that had once nurtured his intellectual growth. The rejection may also have been important in another way:

> The professor's words recurred to me: "You're a Canadian. You should go to the United States." I realized that I had never before thought of myself as a Canadian.
>
> For in Nova Scotia—and I have since learned that it is much the same everywhere in Canada—we were Nova Scotians first and Canadians only when we applied for jobs or passports, or when a war broke out and the Government wanted an army, and even then they said it was England, not Canada, that needed us.

Perhaps involuntarily, MacLennan was learning to think of himself as a Canadian. He followed the professor's advice and yielded to the urgings of his father, when he enrolled as a doctoral candidate at Princeton, where he was "promised a student fellowship that would pay room, lodging, and research tuition and nothing else."[21]

At Princeton, MacLennan encountered professors trained in the Germanic tradition of detailed textual scholarship rather than in the broader tradition of classical humanism he had learned to admire at Oxford. Somewhat unhappily, he settled down to work on his thesis, a study based on some papyrus documents giving details of life in a provincial Egyptian town, named Oxyrhynchus, during the later years of the Roman Empire. As he pursued his research, he thought he perceived similarities between the authoritarian politics of the waning years of the Empire and the fascism that was gaining ascendency in Europe during the 1930s. He sought to understand the causes behind these developments, and for a time, at Princeton and afterwards, he thought he had found a satisfactory explanation in Marxist thought. In the long run, however, Marx's economic determinism could not be congenial to someone in MacLennan's situation. In his private life, MacLennan wanted to be free of his father's domination; equally, in his relationship to society, he wanted to believe that he could shape his own destiny and was not controlled by impersonal economic forces.

As he had at Oxford, MacLennan supplemented his formal studies with summer travel. In a secondhand Studebaker, he toured most of the northern states; and he carried on his courtship of an American woman, whom he had met on the ship that had brought him back to North America. Dorothy Duncan also had literary ambitions, and she gave MacLennan advice on the novel he had begun to write. At Princeton, he met "some brilliant friends who believed that if anyone refused to recognize that *Ulysses* was the master-novel of the twentieth century, he was unfit to make a literary judgment in a kindergarten." Their influence helped shift MacLennan's interest to fiction, and he reports that "for two years I cramped my style by trying to write like James Joyce."[22] In his first year at Princeton, MacLennan completed a novel, which he called "So All Their Praises." The book was accepted by a New York publisher, but the firm unfortunately went broke almost immediately, and the novel has never been published.

When MacLennan left Princeton in 1935, degree in hand, he still had no prospect of a university position. He returned to his father's house in Halifax, where, as in 1928, an unexpected message arrived. In mid-October, six weeks after the school year had started, MacLennan received an offer to teach classics and history at Lower Canada College in Montreal. He did not want to become a schoolmaster, for he thought his training had prepared him for better things; but at the moment he was grateful for any job. Reluctantly, he took a crucial step in the career that would eventually make him a Canadian national institution.

On the strength of his job at Lower Canada College, MacLennan the next year married Dorothy Duncan. With her encouragement, he continued work on his second novel. "A Man Should Rejoice" was completed in 1937 and went the rounds of New York publishers without success, though several firms showed interest. In the later 1930s, MacLennan did publish several essays in the *Lower Canada College Magazine,* which dealt with European politics, tennis, jazz, the Halifax explosion, and his own visit to Russia in the summer of 1937. Like his early fiction, these essays are stylistic experiments in which MacLennan is groping his way to a personal voice. Incidentally, these early pieces might help to put to rest the idea held by some critics that MacLennan is a natural essayist who was forced by market considerations to become a novelist. At the start of his career, MacLennan was just as uncertain in the essay form as he was in the novel. His later ease of expression was learned by hard and painful effort.

In 1937 and 1938, several events combined to shift the direction of MacLennan's thinking. During the Depression,

it was almost obligatory for a writer to take up pens and typewriter for the Left. I was doing my best in this direction until the summer of 1937 when . . . I went to the Soviet Union, only to return stupefied by man's ability to be conned. For years we of the Left had been exposed to propaganda photos showing happy Russian workers laughing and singing. In all the time I spent in Russia I saw only one man laughing and I was told by the Intourist agent that he was a lunatic.[23]

As a direct result of his trip, MacLennan put aside the Marxism with which he had flirted since his Princeton days.

At about the same time, MacLennan was shown by his wife and by the comments of a publisher's reader that his second novel lacked an authoritative sense of place. MacLennan arrived at a decision that he later projected onto Paul Tallard in *Two Solitudes.* He concluded that he must write about the people and places he knew best, even if this decision threatened to limit his readership. MacLennan's decision to write about Canada was also helped by the awareness he gained during a summer visit to Nova Scotia in 1938, "that I had unwittingly acquired a new point of view."[24] Without realizing what was happening, MacLennan had come to think of himself as a Canadian. He would soon celebrate this new identity in his first two published novels.

MacLennan's literary development will be considered in detail in the chapters that follow. At this point, a brief summary of his career will be sufficient. During the years in which he wrote *Barometer Rising* and *Two Solitudes,* MacLennan kept his job at Lower Canada College. His only break came in the winter of 1943–44, when he held a Guggenheim Fellowship to work on the novel that became *Two Solitudes.* In 1945, however, the success of his two novels emboldened MacLennan to leave schoolmastering for the precarious life of a free-lance writer. During the period when he supported himself solely by his writing, MacLennan wrote two novels. *The Precipice,* with its prominent use of American settings, was an attempt to break into the large American market. When this attempt failed, MacLennan returned in *Each Man's Son* to the use of a Canadian setting.

By 1951, then, MacLennan had published four novels. He had a reputation, but little money. He still felt like "another young man with my way to make."[25] The pressure of meeting the medical bills resulting from his wife's recurrent illnesses, brought on by the aftereffects of childhood rheumatic fever, led MacLennan to seek a part-time position in the English department at McGill University. Throughout the fifties he also kept up a steady flow of journalism, including regular columns for the *Montrealer* and *Saturday Night.* At the same time, he worked on his next novel, *The Watch That Ends the Night,* which he completed in a five-month burst of creative effort following his wife's death in the spring of 1957.

Well into the 1970s, MacLennan continued to teach at McGill, having become a full-time member of the teaching faculty in 1964. During this period, he published two more novels, *Return of the Sphinx* and *Voices in Time.* He continued to write occasional articles, usually produced in response to an invitation to review the current state of one of the issues with which he had become identified. He was now one of the country's literary elder statesmen, and honorary degrees and prizes flowed in his direction. MacLennan officially retired from McGill in 1979, but for several years he continued to teach one course. He and his second wife spend their winters in Montreal and their summers at a cottage in North Hatley in Quebec's Eastern Townships.

Letters to a Dead Man

MacLennan was deeply affected by the death of his father on 17 February 1939. To understand his reaction, we must take into account the state of his career at this time. In early 1939, MacLennan was almost thirty-two years old. He had achieved the Rhodes Scholarship and the doctorate that his father had wished him to obtain. But these accomplishments were intended as the prelude to a career that had not materialized. Instead of obtaining the university position for which he had trained, MacLennan was a mere schoolmaster, rehearsing Latin grammar for the unappreciative sons of well-to-do Montreal families. MacLennan had tried to make his mark as a writer, but neither his poems nor his novels had reached print. His Calvinistic sense of his own unworthiness was surely exacerbated by this arrested literary career. In his own eyes and—or so he must have felt—in the eyes of his father, MacLennan was so far a failure.

By dying when he did, Dr. Sam seemed to trap his son. MacLennan had long ago thoroughly assimilated his father's standards and would continue to impose those standards on himself; those efforts would be vindicated when *Barometer Rising* was published to largely favorable reviews. At the time of his father's death, however, MacLennan could not know that this would happen. And suppose he did achieve a future success? How could he communicate the news to someone who was no longer in the world? He seemed locked into his status as a failure.

MacLennan's feeling that his relationship with his father was unsatisfactory and incomplete is strikingly revealed in a series of six letters he wrote in the months following his father's death.[26] MacLennan addressed these letters to his father, calling him "Dadden," just as he had during his father's life. The first two, written in quick succession, are directly personal. In the first letter, MacLennan tells his father: "You are as much alive to me now as you ever were. It is a strange thing, yet very true. Not yourself, not the you that could perform operations, but the you that has always stood in a part—perhaps in the central part—of my mind." MacLennan immediately mentions that a publisher is currently showing interest in "A Man Should Rejoice." He remarks, "I could have wished that you might have at least seen that letter." MacLennan still needs to reinforce his sense of his own worth with the approval of an external source.

MacLennan's sense of being trapped in a situation he cannot control is reinforced by what he sees happening in the world around him. He feels that international politics are creating a world in which the individual is powerless to affect the course of events. He writes: "I am largely what you made me. In a society—at peace—even in a society in the throes of a great struggle towards a better world—I would be able to take my place. I would be able to fulfil your best hopes of your son." MacLennan does not reproach his father, but plainly he feels squeezed between his father's expectations and external events. He continues: "Now, with Caesars within & without, there is only a small place for the individual. It seems to me, therefore, that ambition is largely an illusion. To do a small job such as I have, to do any job at all, as well as I can, is about enough." MacLennan feels the world is denying him his chance. He wants to shift the blame for his apparent failure onto forces outside himself.

In the second letter, MacLennan responds to the imminence of war by drawing an unexpected parallel between himself and his father: "Somehow I feel I can face this future with more courage now than I previously could. I, like yourself, am one of those who have apparently been predestined to have the task of clearing up the messes of other people." The desire to secure approval from his father is clearly behind this comparison. MacLennan then makes a somewhat surprising admission: "If conscripted, I shall use every influence to avoid the fighting forces." But his continuation shows that the desire to avoid combat duty comes from a wish to emulate his father's role as a healer, or if he cannot be a healer, he will at least provide service to others: "The prospect of losing my own life does not affect me so much as does the degradation of being put in the position where it would be my 'duty' to take that of another man. That prospect frankly does appal me. So, possibly a job in the Army Service Corps or the Medical might be arranged—more probably the former."

The concluding paragraph of this letter shows how acutely MacLennan feels that the world is denying him an opportunity to prove himself. He also includes his wife as someone who is thwarted by a world in chaos: "Dorothy is well. We are both on the threshold of the careers for which we planned & trained. An inch more & we will be over it. But meantime the great Question-Mark throws its shadow." As MacLennan puts it in the next letter, the world now lives under a "suspended sentence." He tells his father: "You are well out of it. The international situation unnerves us all; it overshadows every moment of our lives. It makes any important venture, every dream of progress, most of the things men live by, almost impossible."

The later letters are mainly given over to meditations on European politics, specifically to gloomy speculations about the likelihood that no possible diplomatic maneuvers can avert the coming war. These meditations are, of course, an expression of the concern for civilization that Dr. Sam taught his son. But even the political speculations are part of MacLennan's attempt to come to terms with his deceased father. According to Cameron, MacLennan's letters continue a series of conversations he had with his father shortly before Dr. Sam's death.[27] He is trying to show his father that, in a world on the verge of cataclysm, no one is able to shape his own destiny.

The last letter, written after the outbreak of open war, returns to MacLennan's literary concerns. Again he refers to his novel, which the publisher Longmans, Green has by now declined to publish:

In *Man Should Rejoice* I seem to have built a little better than I knew. The book is still unpublished; if the war is lost by mankind it never will be published. But some time, if the war is won, it yet may take its place at full stature, and be understood, although at the time it was originally offered for sale its real meaning was misunderstood even by publishers. Its main view of life, understood intuitively by me during those hectic years after I left Oxford, has now been corroborated by the things which have happened.

For even in 1934, when the book was conceived, I understood that the evils of the time were occasioned by unbridled science. I knew that the indifference of scientists to anything except objective success in a limited field had permitted quasi-scientists to have dreams of magalomania [*sic*].

Ostensibly, MacLennan is simply congratulating himself on his astuteness in perceiving that science and technology are the major determinants of twentieth-century history. But this self-praise is addressed to "Dadden." Again MacLennan is offering his novel as evidence that he has met his father's standards.

Two years later he continued to propitiate his father's spirit by dedicating *Barometer Rising* "to the memory of my father." Indeed, all of MacLennan's fiction is addressed to "Dadden" and constitutes an attempt to prove that Dr. Sam's son did amount to something in the world.

Family Romances

A particularly striking feature of MacLennan's novels is his depiction of families and, above all, his portrayal of a memorable series of encounters between fathers and sons. MacLennan's fictional treatment of fathers and sons is directly related to his own upbringing, which left him with strongly ambivalent feelings toward his father. For a long time, he was unable to acknowledge the antagonism that was an integral part of his close attachment to Dr. Sam. Nonetheless, this feeling strongly influenced his portrayal of fictional relationships between fathers and sons. In his novels, MacLennan creates strict and oppressive fathers whose shortcomings are exposed and who in some cases are subjected to catastrophic violence. When he inflicts punishment on his fictional fathers or puts them in a bad light, he is indirectly expressing feelings he can utter in no other way.

Whether MacLennan consciously meant to, he has used his fiction to define and eventually to resolve some of his own deepest inner conflicts. It seems very likely that MacLennan's father provoked the divided response that Freud discusses in his important essay "Family Romances."[28] "For a small child," Freud writes, "his parents are at first the only authority and the source of all belief." As the child develops, he necessarily realizes that his parents are not all-powerful; moreover, he cannot avoid incurring the parents' occasional disapproval. As a result, the child may create fantasies in which his real parents are replaced by other parents who better fit the child's conception of what parents should be.

Such feelings appear to exist in MacLennan and are frequently expressed in his work by the use of plots in which children lose one set of parents and gain surrogates. MacLennan typically places his fictional sons between opposing father figures, one a stern oppressor and the other an indulgent and approving adviser. Often, the stern fathers are destroyed, so that the young man is conveniently relieved of the responsibility of trying to please an impossibly demanding taskmaster. On the other hand, the kindly surrogate father usually extends a love that does not have to be earned but instead is given without condition or qualification. Usually, too, the sexuality of the oppressive parent is clearly apparent, and the sexuality of the kindly father figure is not emphasized. By turning to the surrogate father, MacLennan's protagonists are trying to avoid confronting the oedipal hostility existing between father and son; but their efforts are only partially successful. Unresolved oedipal tensions underlie a number of vividly rendered primal scenes scattered throughout MacLennan's fiction. In these scenes, which are sometimes presented directly and sometimes presented in symbolic form, parental sexuality is lined with the emotions that have driven a father and son into destructive conflict. Thus, MacLennan's fiction frequently builds its superstructure of realistically portrayed action on a foundation of universal childhood fantasies.

This being so, it is useful to remember something else Freud said concerning family romances. Freud reminds his readers "that these works of fiction, which seem so full of hostility, are none of them so badly intended, and that they still preserve, under a slight disguise, the child's original affection for his parents." He goes on to say, "The whole effort at replacing the real father by a superior one is only an expression of the child's longing for the happy, vanished days when his father seemed to him the noblest and strongest of men and his mother the dearest and loveliest of women." This lyrical passage, which finds a nostalgia for childhood security beneath fantasies that appear to show hostility to parental figures, can readily serve as a description of MacLennan's fiction. Indeed, most of his novels contain an idyllic place of retreat that really embodies an idealized vision of childhood. When he turns to the larger social world within which his characters move, MacLennan always tries to illuminate the underlying forces directing political and economic events. However, his portrayal of the individual's relationship to the external world is frequently modeled on the relationship of a child to an arbitrary and powerful parent. He habitually sees national or collective psychology as extensions of individual psychology, and he often understands national and international politics as family dynamics writ large. Moreover, the Calvinism that MacLennan portrays so vividly is dominated by a punitive, authoritarian God who is a magnified image of the authoritarian fathers that dominate most of his fictional families. Therefore, the social and religious dimensions of MacLennan's fiction are often simply enlarged versions of his recurrent subject, the patriarchal family.

Chapter Two
Young Men of 1933

As MacLennan watched the course of international politics throughout the 1930s, he was dismayed. Current events seemed to move with an inner logic of their own, inexorably pushing the world toward a confrontation that could only be disastrous. MacLennan found himself forced into a deterministic outlook; yet he desperately wanted to believe in the continued possibility of individual freedom. His desire to reconcile the political realities of the thirties with the aspirations he still cherished for the individual provided a central theme for his two unpublished novels, and even helped to shape the conclusions he drew in his doctoral dissertation.

For a closer look at MacLennan's dilemma, we can examine the literary efforts of Paul Tallard in *Two Solitudes,* which are modeled on MacLennan's own literary apprenticeship. Paul's novel is called "Young Man of 1933." The title refers to the year in which Hitler came to power; yet Hitler is not the ultimate cause of the social upheaval Paul is describing. Hitler, the power-hungry madman, is only the most spectacular symptom of a far-reaching social revolution. The real instigator of the new outlook is the machine, for the technological mentality turns people into statistics and treats them as components in a vast social engineering project. In a society built around the machine, Paul reflects, "the still small voice of God the Father [is] no longer audible through the stroke of the connecting rod." Paul faces a dilemma that also confronted MacLennan at this time. Paul tells himself that "a novel should concern people, not ideas, and yet people had become trivial."[1]

"So All Their Praises"

In "So All Their Praises," his first attempt at fiction, MacLennan tried to write a tough-minded "proletarian" novel about two young men whose lives have been blighted by the Depression.[2] The main characters are the

German student Adolph Fabricius and his English friend Michael Carmichael. Both youths have been thwarted by social forces beyond their control—they are both "young men of 1933." Their story begins in Germany, where Adolph and Michael find themselves caught up in the deteriorating economic conditions of the early 1930s. Adolph graduates from university in 1929 and celebrates by formally announcing his engagement to his girlfriend Hilda. Two years later he still has not found a job. As a result, he postpones his marriage and eventually breaks off the engagement. His sense of failure leads him to a suicide attempt from which he is rescued by Michael. For a short time Adolph and Michael work sporadically at manual labor; but when no more work can be found, they obtain passage to North America aboard a Nova Scotia rumrunner, the *Martin Swicker*.

Adolph and Michael provide the first instance of a frequent MacLennan technique, the use of doubled characters. By using this device, MacLennan is able to explore both sides of an issue without committing himself to a single answer, or he can present both sides of an emotional conflict without being forced to present a single, simplified outcome. Both young men are in conflict with their fathers, but their contrasting temperaments make them respond in different ways. Adolph is a serious, introverted young man, who feels humiliated by his failure to begin a career. He has internalized his father's expectations and judges himself harshly, even though his failure to secure a job is no fault of his own, but the result of economic conditions. In contrast, Michael has rejected the bourgeois standards of his lawyer father and welcomes the marginal existence as itinerant workers that he and Adolph briefly adopt. Michael feels that he can eventually turn his experiences into subject matter for fiction. Adolph, on the other hand, feels degraded by manual labor.

When Adolph and Michael sail to America, their ostensible purpose is to find work, but in the final analysis they are both trying to run away from themselves. Instead of seeking work ashore, they slide easily into jobs aboard the smuggling ship. When the *Martin Swicker* puts into Halifax after discharging its cargo somewhere off the New England coast, Michael meets the Scottish girl Sarah MacRae. Michael in turn introduces Adolph to Sarah, and it is the earnest and rather inhibited Adolph who ultimately becomes romantically linked with her. On a picnic just before the two men are to sail again, Adolph falls—quite literally—into an unexpected sexual encounter with Sarah. When the two men resume their smuggling activities, Adolph and Sarah continue their relationship by letter.

Eventually it appears that the bootlegging syndicate for which the ship has been working is about to betray them to the American customs officials. Before this can happen, however, the ship's captain is persuaded to steal the cargo and embark on a private smuggling operation. In the interludes of shore rest in New York between smuggling voyages, Michael enrolls in some university courses and both men become part of a loosely organized group devoted to the discussion of socialist ideas. Finally the smuggling enterprise comes to an end when the American contact man runs off with the profits. Adolph and Michael are again left nearly destitute, having gained only whatever wisdom their experiences have brought them.

Just before this happens, Adolph receives word that his father is dying. He returns to Germany and is reconciled with his father, who in old age is frail and no longer an intimidating figure. Indeed, Adolph's father has become almost ethereal in appearance, and his time is given over to philosophical musings. The death of his father frees Adolph to embark on his own life. He comments that the funeral "will be like burying twenty-four years of my life, for up to that time I was only a branch of him." He returns to New York, where Sarah joins him. They make plans to be married and earn their living by managing a fruit farm in the Annapolis valley of Nova Scotia.

Michael's fate is not as clearly defined as Adolph's. He takes passage on a ship to England, where presumably he plans to re-establish contact with his family. The final incident in the novel takes place aboard ship. One evening Michael spends a long time leaning precariously over the ship's railing. He is approached by a stranger, who turns out to be a reformed alcoholic. This good samaritan insists on talking with Michael in the belief that Michael is on the point of jumping overboard. Michael's attitude to his benefactor is unclear. He mocks the man's simple religious beliefs, but nonetheless carries on a long conversation with him. By the end of the conversation, it is apparent that Michael will not commit suicide, whatever his previous intentions may have been. In the concluding passage of the novel, Michael pretentiously alludes to *King Lear* when he describes himself as "God's spy." He feels his insight into the world around him will forever separate him from other people. "Little Michael must get used to talking to himself," he says. "He won't be wanting to have many more friends." The reader is surely meant to recognize that Michael's self-pity is excessive. But whether this final passage represents shallow cynicism or the beginnings of wisdom is not clear.

"So All Their Praises" is very much an apprentice work. The basic story, describing the initiation of youth into the adult world, is typical of first novels. The self-conscious experiments with style show a writer just beginning to learn the possibilities of his medium. Many aspects of the writing are out of focus. For example, the most extensive descriptions depict Nova Scotia, yet the most significant action takes place in Germany and the United States. There is an inherent implausibility about much of the book's action. Though it is plain that the plot is designed to illustrate the breakdown of society, MacLennan never quite faces the moral ambiguity of having his two main characters turn into Prohibition-era bootleggers. (Perhaps he simply sees no problem; he is well aware that smuggling has had a long history in Nova Scotia and has been viewed as almost a legitimate form of commercial enterprise.)

The book has conspicuous weaknesses of both structure and technique. The structural problems come about because the personal problems of the characters are never adequately integrated with the social context in which the action takes place. The emotional center of gravity in the book lies in the love story and in the conflicts of the young men with their fathers. But the events that deal with these themes are almost completely divorced from the events that carry the book's social message that economic and political forces distort the lives of individuals. Moreover, MacLennan's sympathies appear to shift as the novel progresses. At the outset, the aspiring writer Michael is the main center of consciousness. Gradually the emotional awakening of Adolph takes over as the main action, but at the end of the story MacLennan rather abruptly returns his attention to Michael's development.

Stylistically, the novel shows an uneasy mixture of influences. MacLennan says he admired James Joyce during his Princeton years; however, the Joycean influence is not as obvious in "So All Their Praises" as is that of Ernest Hemingway. This sentence from the novel's opening paragraph will serve as an illustration:

It was comfortable in the drinking room, for the company was warm with wine and good feeling and everyone felt voluptuously friendly towards the others and was very conscious that they were all young together and that the world was in a bad way and that they were the ones who would make the world right.

The sentence structure—short main clauses joined by a series of coordinate conjunctions—is modeled on Hemingway's style, as is the detached and slightly cynical narrative mood. But MacLennan's sentence departs from

Hemingway's technique in that MacLennan uses generalizations and a judgmental vocabulary (for example, *voluptuously*), whereas Hemingway uses particular details, neutrally presented.

If there is a Joycean influence present in the novel, it comes in the occasional paragraphs that venture into stream-of-consciousness narrative. The book is written in the third person, past tense, but in scenes of emotional crisis MacLennan sometimes inserts paragraphs written in the first person, present tense. These passages attempt to capture the associative flow of a character's spontaneous thoughts, as in the account of Adolph's thoughts as he walks with Hilda on the evening their engagement has been announced:

> I feel her hand warm about my body, lumbar muscles rising and falling, falling and rising with compulsion under clothing, two bodies moving rhythmically, swaying forward slowly, waves following each other into a shore. Scent of hair, of leaves decaying in the nearer Black Forest hills. Freiburg, Freiburg-im-Breisgau, of the Holy Roman Empire and still very Catholic. The knight rose from prayer before the tapers in the Dom, got up from his knees reverently and turned in time to see his shadow leap to the roof. He smelled the emptiness of the cathedral, then left and walked down the row of priests' houses in the Herrnstrasse to the painted Schwabentor and so to the road that left the city, to do something not for its own sake or for himself.

The sudden leap into the consciousness of a medieval knight-errant certainly draws attention to Adolph's naive romanticism, and a Joycean ironic parallel between present and past is achieved. But the literary device is too obvious here; the passage draws attention to the author's attempt to be clever more than it illuminates features of Adolph's mind.

In the light of MacLennan's subsequent career, it is interesting to examine the way he presents Nova Scotia as an idyllic contrast with the troubled conditions in Germany and America. His descriptions of the Nova Scotian landscape anticipate some of the descriptive sections of *Barometer Rising,* and the political role he attributes to Nova Scotia also foreshadows ideas expressed in the later novel. At one point Sarah MacRae says:

> "I sometimes feel that this continent does not civilize easily. Of course, I don't really know about the States. Canada, and in particular this little province, seems to be just half way between the Old Country and the States. I think that there is more intensity in the States and better balance here."

These ideas are not corroborated by any detailed portrayal of Nova Scotian society. The passage gives evidence of the nostalgic glow MacLennan was beginning to cast over his native province, but artistically it is an intrusion. MacLennan seems unwilling to let the plot of his novel do its work unaided. He intrudes his concern that the individual is powerless to affect the course of history into the speeches of his characters and into the imagery he uses. It is really MacLennan speaking when Adolph remarks, "History always works itself out inexorably and at a late stage in a historical system there is nothing the individual can do to alter the process." Soon afterwards, Adolph reiterates this idea when he compares the "forces of history" influencing the mass of humanity to the moon's gravity heaving the tides about the earth; MacLennan then glosses this image by explaining, "He saw himself in the mass and the mass like the ocean he was on; himself, the individual, subject to accident, but the movement of the mass predetermined." A simple point, already implicit in the book's action, is here being clumsily underlined.

"So All Their Praises" is not directly autobiographical, but it does indirectly reflect MacLennan's situation at the time he was writing the book. Like MacLennan, Adolph and Michael are both haunted by strong fathers, and both seek emotional and financial autonomy. Their story enacts MacLennan's conviction that the Depression has unfairly thwarted the careers of many individuals. When he transforms Adolph's father into an aging and fragile philosopher, MacLennan appears to express his own wish that his father were a less imposing figure. Adolph and Michael act as alter egos for MacLennan. But only Adolph, who seems more distant from MacLennan than does Michael, is allowed a resolution of his difficulties. Michael, the aspiring writer, remains aloof and troubled, a young man with his way still to make.

Yet in the book's final scene, MacLennan may have inserted a poignant personal note. Michael tries to deflate the good samaritan's religious beliefs by implying that God is merely a kind of emotional security blanket: "The Lord, you think, is mindful of his own. A man must believe somehow that he has a father and that the father is not an accident." Michael's words actually describe a perfectly natural human desire to belong to a meaningful universe, in which one is a welcome guest rather than an accidental sojourner. MacLennan gave Michael a speech that embodies the deepest longing of many of his subsequent protagonists—the desire to feel "at home" in the world.

Oxyrhynchus and "Roman History and To-Day"

Although MacLennan did not succeed in publishing his novel, he did soon manage to get his doctoral dissertation accepted; at about the same time the *Dalhousie Review* accepted two articles based on his doctoral research. In *Oxyrhynchus: A Social and Economic Study,* MacLennan is writing a kind of social history.[3] He wants to identify the underlying patterns behind historical events and describe the forces that shaped the individuals who lived in the society he is describing. By studying the thesis and the two articles derived from it, we can learn something of MacLennan's intellectual position during the middle 1930s.

MacLennan describes the people of Oxyrhynchus as Aristotelian materialists, seeking fulfillment through worldly success. He is very interested in what happens when these materialists find that material success is denied them: "By the close of the third century, the environment of the Greeks in Egypt had so altered that the conditions required to satisfy an Aristotelian philosophy had for most of them become impossible" (82). The poor and disadvantaged, in particular, came to believe "that self-realization in the present world was not feasible" (82). As a result, they were readily converted to the Christian religion, which promised them an other-worldly salvation.

MacLennan's account of the development of Christianity in *Oxyrhynchus* is not flattering. He remarks:

> It is commonly thought that the coming of Christianity was a blessing to the people and for a generation it undoubtedly was. In later times, however, those to whom the religion could be made profitable do not appear to have themselves been sources of blessing to others. The earlier confessors had sought recompense for a hopeless existence, and some had attained it, but their descendants were left with a fortune still worse and with tangible evidence that the acceptance of the new religion had not altered the acquisitive instincts of those in power. (83)

By the ninth century, the Church had become a wealthy landowner; and, as MacLennan sardonically remarks: "Here, as elsewhere, the spirit of brotherly affection was incompatible with the acquisition of excessive power by small minorities" (90).

MacLennan also proposes what may be in his eyes an even more fundamental criticism of the Church: it contributed to the decay of classical culture. He puts his argument in terminology that seems to indicate at least a secondhand acquaintance with Freudian ideas. "While no one would question the fact of belief at this date," he writes, "the psychological nature of it requires some qualification" (86). Christians meditated upon Christ's sufferings and perhaps identified their own suffering with his. As a result:

the habit of thinking in masochistic symbols appeared, and in the ancient world this was something new. To identify the self with the object of suffering was foreign to the whole spirit of classicism. . . . On the other hand, masochism is the very essence of thought in the Dark Ages. If this development is traceable to Christianity, then it can truly be said that it was Christianity which dealt the ancient culture its final death-blow, because it robbed mankind of its will to rely on reason and to value the power of the intellect. (87)

Psychoanalytic thought was not the only outside influence on MacLennan's thinking at this time. His interest in Marx is implicit in the importance he attributes to economic factors in determining the quality of life in Oxyrhynchus. But apparently Princeton was not the place to submit a Marxist thesis. MacLennan's Marxist perspective is more openly presented in a later article, in which he explicitly describes the Roman Empire as "a society founded on the principle of private enterprise," and interprets the decline of the Empire as evidence of the intrinsic weakness of capitalism. "The history of this town [Oxyrhynchus]" he writes, "is the history of the Decline and Fall seen through the large end of the telescope, and it shows conclusively that although private enterprise was responsible for the greatness of Rome, it was also responsible for the reduction of democratic communities to a quasi-feudal serfdom."[4]

Although *Oxyrhynchus* is an academic dissertation, MacLennan's introduction makes it plain that he wishes to do more than enumerate certain facts of ancient history. He wishes to make his research apply to the modern world. The introduction begins, "The growth and collapse of the Roman Empire . . . presents to us now, as it has presented to all generations since the Renascence, a series of questions which somehow must be solved if our own culture is to survive" (9). However, in his dissertation MacLennan was not free to meditate at length upon the present significance of his findings. Instead, he put his reflections into another article, "Roman History and To-Day," which became the first of his many attempts to analyze the course of civilization in our own time.[5]

In this article, MacLennan urges historians to "venture out of the study into the open forum." In a troubled era, he wants scholars to take on social responsibility, not retreat into their ivory towers. "The personal attitude of the present writer," he says, "is the not uncommon belief that we have reached the end of an era, though not of our civilization; and that the history of the Romans, whose vast civilization reached an end *for itself,* can throw much light on our own predicament to-day." His comments also show that his methods as well as his purposes differ from those of a dry-as-dust textual scholar or antiquarian. He insists that "the *tone* of many documents in the Oxyrhynchus papyri . . . is as valuable as the actual content." But psychology is still a relatively primitive discipline; therefore, he argues that "the mind best adapted to draw inferences from such data is the artist's." In these comments the young classical historian and the apprentice novelist converge; indeed, their purposes are virtually identical.

In the conclusion of his article, MacLennan suggests that modern technology may offer a way out of the impasse that faced the later Roman Empire. The citizens of Imperial Rome found themselves subordinated to an increasingly organized state; they became, in effect, slaves to the needs of the imperial bureaucracy. Today, "machines provide a means of decreasing the necessity of slavery in the world." But MacLennan's optimism is tempered by a warning that a change of outlook is also necessary: "Unless state-education is altered and the values of the masses are profoundly altered, the new era will not escape the old vicious circle." The "vicious circle" to which he refers is the alternation between periods of democratic freedom, which decline into chaos, and periods of authoritarian rule, which initially are welcomed as antidotes to the confusion into which the previous democratic period has declined. MacLennan sees the Roman emperors as analogous to the fascist leaders who were coming to power in Europe at the time he was writing.

By completing his doctorate, MacLennan accomplished the program his father had laid down for him. Yet the attitude he takes toward religion can be seen as a rebellion against his father's religious position. MacLennan appears to see religion as a response to social pressures acting on the individual; surely a certain amount of skepticism is involved in suggesting that a people's religion can be interpreted by examining their psychological and material conditions. But in a larger sense, MacLennan's academic writings carry out his father's purposes, for they show MacLennan upholding the classical values upon which his education was based.

MacLennan's historical researches leave him still suspended between determinism and free will. In "Roman History and To-Day," he insists that "in these days of intellectual bewilderment" the historian's ability to discern and describe a pattern in the past "must necessarily help to explain our own society to ourselves." Yet whether he thinks humanity can actually break out of the "vicious circle" is not clear. Thanks to the work of modern social analysts, "the process of events is seen, with pitiless clarity, to be issuing from formal causes far remote." It may be that historical events are shaped by forces over which humanity can exercise no control.

"A Man Should Rejoice"

MacLennan's second attempt at fiction, "A Man Should Rejoice," is a considerable advance on his first effort.[6] It is a more ambitious novel, nearly twice as long as its predecessor, and is more polished in style and construction. Here MacLennan drops the attempt to imitate Hemingway's style and outlook. Indeed, during the writing of the novel, he predicted in a letter to his friend George Barrett, "Inside a few years the Hemingway school will be a back number." In the same letter, he deprecated those American writers who respond to a world they see as "rotten" simply by "swimming up and down sewers saying how tough they are." MacLennan's own goal, he tells Barrett, is to take a more balanced, less fatalistic look at the ongoing social upheaval:

> We belong to the transition, and to me that's all there is to it. . . . the question is, can a human being have and feel significance when he lives in such an age? Frankly I don't know, though I do believe it is not impossible. The book I am now doing will be a statement on that question, but a statement from one individual only.[7]

By the time he wrote this letter, MacLennan was well embarked on "A Man Should Rejoice." This book is narrated in the first person by David Culver, a young man who has done much and suffered much, and is now writing down his story in order to clarify its significance both to himself and to the reader. The first part of the novel tells the story of David's childhood. His father is Bernard Culver, an engineer and businessman. His mother is Arina, a Russian woman whom Bernard meets while serving as a technical adviser to a Russian mining venture. The marriage is not a success. Bernard Culver understands only utilitarian values, whereas Arina values cultural attainments above all else. David grows up torn between his parents' opposing values. His father tolerates David's artistic interests only as a childish hobby and assumes that when David matures he will put away childish things, attend university, and eventually enter business. Arina has quite a different plan for David's life. At a point when David is debating whether to work for his father, she tells him: "I've looked forward for twenty-three years to when you would become a man. . . . You would be a famous artist and people in London and Paris would point out your work and we would go away from here and be happy." David says of his father: "I hate everything he stands for. Not only the way he mechanizes life but every damn thing he does to achieve it. It's death." Nonetheless, David does go to work for his father, after taking a one-year detour to study art in Paris. His idea is that before he can launch out for himself, he must learn enough about his father to be able to confront him on equal terms.

David has never been intimate with his father, who spends most of his time in Pittsburgh, while David and his mother live in a country house. David says that a sympathetic neighbor, Edward Eisenhardt, "was the nearest approach to a father I ever had." Eisenhardt has made enough money to live comfortably in retirement; he sees business only as a means, not as an end in itself. He gives David the affection and guidance his father fails to provide. Eisenhardt thus becomes the first of many kindly substitute fathers MacLennan has created. Eisenhardt's own adopted son Nicholas becomes David's closest friend. These two figures, like Adolph and Michael, are an instance of MacLennan's penchant for creating paired characters who have contrasting personalities. David is introspective and studies art; Nicholas is pragmatic and studies engineering.

After working for a year at one of his father's rolling mills, David moves to an oil refinery, where the degree in chemistry he has unwillingly acquired may be of some use. In the meantime he has become, in theory at least, a Communist. He arranges the hiring of Nicholas, now a Communist organizer, as a workman at the refinery, and he connives at planning a strike which the party leaders see as part of their campaign to overthrow American capitalism. The contradictions within David's position are obvious. He is a rich man's son and also a Communist; he earns his living by serving technology but wishes to become an artist. In short, he has not decided whether he will live his own life or will acquiesce to his father's plan.

While the strike is being planned, David is also carrying on a romance with Anne Lawrence, a girl he met during his year in Europe.[8] On the eve of the strike, David breaks with the party when he cannot accept an unquestioning obedience to its commands as the proper course of action. He marries Anne. During the actual attempt to organize the strike, they are away on their honeymoon. In fact, the strike never takes place, for a clever and ambitious engineer, who appeared to sympathize with the rebellious workmen, now betrays their plans to company officials.

Nicholas is arrested, tried, and convicted; David is later convicted of perjuring himself at Nicholas's trial. David's trial marks a final break with his father, for the trial takes place at the express order of Bernard Culver, who announces that he no longer regards David as his son. After a year's imprisonment, David emerges as a nearly broken man. Gradually, however, the patience and love of his wife bring him back to emotional life. His revival is completed when he and Anne return to the small Austrian village of Lorbeerstein, where David had first met her. This village, run on socialist principles, has so far escaped the worst effects of the economic and political chaos that is sweeping over Europe. Yet its prosperity is fragile, for, as David says, Lorbeerstein is only "a kernel of sanity and gentleness alive still on a doomed continent." In Lorbeerstein David approaches happiness when his wife becomes pregnant and his paintings are exhibited by a Vienna art dealer. But the political forces that are conspiring to seize power in Austria put an end to this idyllic interlude. The village is attacked and among the victims of the fighting is David's wife, who is killed before his horrified eyes in the first of MacLennan's recurrent scenes of explosive violence.

After the battle David is taken prisoner. Although wounded, he escapes and struggles through the snowy countryside to the nearby monastery of Saint Johann. There, in a conversation with the father superior, he is given the spiritual consolation that enables him to go on living and to persevere in his career as a painter. "As a man grows older," the superior says, "if he is a good man he comes slowly into a perception of the eternal. That is what is happening to you." The superior tells David: "You don't have to believe in any miracles at all. You only have to believe there are more good people in the world than evil and know that they will always be your friends." David tells the reader: "'Yes,' I said, and my eyes turned to the hills, 'Yes . . .'" This ending does not seem satisfactory. Only the previous day David has witnessed Anne's death. The priest's words do not seem a sufficient answer to the political and social injustice that has preceded them. Thus, David's eventual retreat to Nova Scotia to paint seems to be an evasion of the issues his story has raised.

"A Man Should Rejoice" has other weaknesses. In the story of David's childhood, the emotional conflicts are an integral part of the action, but once David starts to work for his father, some of these emotional conflicts seem extraneous to the social issues that become the book's central concern. David's flirtation with communism can perhaps be defended as necessary to show him that rigid ideology cannot be a solution to the problems he sees in the capitalist society his father represents. But the later excursions into European politics seem awkward and digressive. Lorbeerstein is an unconvincing utopia. Its destruction appears to be introduced in order to make a point about European politics, which have not figured in the novel up to that point.

The two unpublished novels possess some important common features. Both deal with the enforced maturing of young men. Both contrast the detachment of an aspiring artist with the involvement in society of a more earnest and pragmatic figure. In both novels the artist ends in isolation, cut off from all human warmth. MacLennan's presentation of his artists may be superficially influenced by Joyce's *A Portrait of the Artist as a Young Man,* but MacLennan's theme is fundamentally different from Joyce's. Joyce shows Stephen Dedalus choosing to cut himself off from a restrictive society in order to attain artistic autonomy. MacLennan's artists, however, are cut off from society against their will. They are the involuntary victims of impersonal social forces.

By emphasizing the economic and political conditions that affect his main characters, MacLennan obscures their private emotional struggles to assert their own personalities in the face of oppressively strong parental figures. In both novels MacLennan's protagonists are too symbolic, too much the representative "young men of 1933." Indeed, many of MacLennan's characters are one-dimensional embodiments of a particular role or idea. In "A Man Should Rejoice," for example, there is a representative businessman, a power-hungry technocrat, and specimens of both the political idealist and the political fanatic. Moreover, all of MacLennan's female characters are poorly drawn, little more than embodiments of youthful male fantasies.

Both unpublished novels anticipate many motifs that occur in MacLennan's subsequent fiction. With his businessman father and his cultured mother, David Culver resembles Stephen Lassiter of *The Precipice.* Bernard Culver is introduced in terms very similar to those used to describe Huntly McQueen in *Two Solitudes:* "The country has many more brilliant millionaires than Culver, but no sounder ones." However, the most striking anticipations of MacLennan's later fiction are those features of "A Man Should Rejoice" that foreshadow aspects of MacLennan's best novel, *The Watch That Ends the Night.* David Culver is a reflective and cultivated narrator, who writes in measured, eloquent prose. The novel is told retrospectively, as in *The Watch That Ends the Night.* Like George Stewart, David Culver finds himself through the love of a woman and retains only a precarious mental balance when that woman is taken from him. David Culver's observation that political events "seemed totally unimportant, a flash in the pan when compared to the life of the universe" anticipates George Stewart's vision of the material world as a kind of shadow-play obscuring a deeper spiritual reality. However, not until *The Watch That Ends the Night* does MacLennan succeed in providing a convincing portrayal of the redemptive value of suffering.

MacLennan's state of mind as the 1930s drew to a close can be inferred by considering the fate of David Culver. David is torn between parents of very different temperaments and is buffeted by society. The fictional resolution of his problems sees him separated from both parents, turning inward to commune with his own thoughts and adopting a purely formal or esthetic view of art. David's near-solipsism reflects MacLennan's own wish that a troublesome world would leave him alone, though such thoroughgoing quietism could not content him for long at this period of his life. MacLennan's uncertainty is reflected in the fact that "So All Their Praises" and "A Man Should Rejoice" end inconclusively. In both novels, the individual appears to be defeated by external physical or economic forces. Although an implicitly materialistic outlook is reflected in his academic writing, a religious note is sounded at the end of both novels, indicating that MacLennan is still strongly attracted to a nonmaterialist or even a spiritual outlook.

Chapter Three
National Romances

In writing *Barometer Rising,* MacLennan faced a new kind of problem. He had become convinced that he must set his fiction in Canada. Yet he did not find anywhere in Canadian literature a precedent for his own attempt to portray Canadian settings and characters. At this time, the only images that were the common property of both Canadian readers and authors were the clichés and caricatures of popular fiction: from historical romances set in the ancien régime came the haughty seigneur, the decadent intendant, the heroic British conqueror, and the pious habitant; from the northern poems of Robert Service came the hardy trapper and the lonely sourdough; from the novels of Ralph Connor and Robert Stead came the determined prairie settler and his enduring wife. For the serious novelist, MacLennan announced, "there is as yet no tradition of Canadian literature."[1]

MacLennan therefore faced a difficult job of literary pioneering. With no stock of familiar images to draw upon, he would have to invent his literary portrayal of Canada virtually single-handed. Moreover, his potential readers, many of them American, would know very little about Canadian society. Specifically, MacLennan planned to set his story in Halifax. To do so would involve depicting characters whose attitudes were shaped by a long and eventful local history. Knowledge of this history was essential in order to prevent readers from interpreting Nova Scotian society as simply a replica of either British or American society. It was plain to MacLennan that he would have to educate his readers as he told his story. Like his later alter ego Paul Tallard in *Two Solitudes,* "He could afford to take nothing for granted. He would have to build the stage and props for his play, and then write the play itself."[2]

As MacLennan thought about his task, he debated how best to impart the necessary local knowledge to his readers. His solution in *Barometer Rising* has been the subject of much critical debate. He chose to incorporate the expository passages that many later readers have found intrusive and overly didactic. Later he also included similar passages in *Two Solitudes* and *The Precipice*. MacLennan wrote in this manner because he felt that the only way to make his stories fully intelligible to his readers was, in effect, to include a series of historical and sociological notes within the texts of his novels. Similar passages can be found in many novels recognized as world classics. The valid criticism of MacLennan's technique is not that his expository passages are inadmissible in fiction but that too often his use of exposition is clumsy. Despite their flaws, however, MacLennan's first two published novels have a significant place in the history of Canadian fiction.

Barometer Rising

When he began *Barometer Rising*, MacLennan wanted very much to write a successful novel. To make his book salable, he made sure the action built to an impressive climax, and he organized the story around a dramatic event, the Halifax explosion. At the novel's center he put a sentimental love story with the shape of a traditional fairy tale. *Barometer Rising* tells the story of a wronged stepson, long presumed dead, who returns to life and wins the beautiful daughter of the wicked stepfather.

Although written and published in the early years of World War II, MacLennan's novel is set in the First World War. It is therefore a kind of historical novel, and like most historical fiction since Sir Walter Scott's day, it presents the vicissitudes of two star-crossed lovers against the background of a momentous historical event. The strength of MacLennan's novel lies where it often does in historical romances, in the depiction of the background and the portrayal of secondary characters. The novel's weakness also lies in the usual place, in the lack of substance in the nominal hero and heroine and in the lack of organic connection between the love story and the historical background.

With the creation of Neil Macrae, MacLennan moved away from the quietism that ends both of his unpublished novels. The emphasis in *Barometer Rising* falls on external action, not on inner reflection. MacLennan accordingly abandoned the first-person narration he had tried in "A Man Should Rejoice" and used an omniscient point of view. At different points in the novel, he uses Neil Macrae, Penny Wain, Angus Murray, Colonel Wain, and Roddy Wain as centers of consciousness. However, he makes little attempt to adjust his language to the personality of the character whose thoughts he is describing. In some passages, notably in the account of the explosion, he also employs an all-seeing narrator who is clearly a native Haligonian, familiar with the city's geography, history, and typical weather patterns.

MacLennan's choice of technique is pragmatic. He simply wants to get on with his story in the most convenient way available. He is not concerned with adhering to the fine points of some particular theory of fiction. As he writes, the social and political dimensions of the events he is narrating are uppermost in his mind. Throughout the novel, MacLennan's approach is doggedly earnest. There is little irony or humor in *Barometer Rising*. Only the preposterous speeches of Uncle Alfred and Aunt Maria are allowed to stand without comment as self-evidently ridiculous. Often the narrator delivers summaries which tell the reader how to interpret events or how to assess a character's opinions, and many of the ideas expressed by the characters are clearly echoes of the author's viewpoint. Only Colonel Wain consistently expresses incorrect judgments, and his credibility is undermined not only by his obvious moral corruption but by the direct contradiction of other characters. For instance, Angus Murray tells him, "At least your notion of a military dictatorship in this country is a lot of balls" (156).

MacLennan's technique is not subtle, but in a sense his narrative method does reinforce the novel's themes. The physical action of *Barometer Rising* is worked out within a carefully re-created local geography, and events are assigned places in a precise chronology. The pivotal event of the book—the Halifax explosion and its aftermath—is described with historically verifiable exactness. The book's framework is documentary: each day is allotted a separate chapter, and hourly intervals demarcate the subdivisions within chapters. In short, the narrative method is implicitly deterministic, emphasizing the external forces against which the characters struggle. This is entirely appropriate in a novel dealing with characters hemmed about with political and social restrictions.

The characters in *Barometer Rising* are assigned to the family roles that are given prominence throughout MacLennan's fiction: Neil Macrae and Roddy Wain are sons; Penny Wain is a daughter; Colonel Wain is a father; and Angus Murray, the kindly and avuncular helper, is really a father in disguise. The generational conflict that pits Neil and Penny against Colonel Wain also takes on additional political significance in this novel. Colonel Wain represents the colonial-minded old order, which has for so long held Canadians in bondage to Britain. "Everything in this damn country is second-rate," he tells Murray. "It always is, in a colony" (151). On the other hand, Neil Macrae's determination to regain his own identity makes him the representative of the new-found maturity and self-confidence of younger Canadians.

As the novel opens, Neil Macrae has returned to Halifax to claim his identity. To do this he must refute the charges of cowardice brought by Colonel Wain. The novel's success therefore ought to hang to a considerable extent on the effectiveness with which the confrontation between these two characters is presented. Here an obvious deficiency in MacLennan's plotting becomes apparent. Neil and Colonel Wain never confront each other directly. In fact, they meet only when Neil discovers the body of the colonel, who has been killed in his mistress's apartment by the explosion. The ending has, as MacLennan has acknowledged, a deus ex machina quality.[3] The outcome is entirely too convenient for Neil, who never has to demonstrate his mettle in direct opposition to the colonel. Moreover, the evidence that will presumably vindicate Neil is collected by Angus Murray, not by Neil himself.

The reader's belief in Neil must therefore rest on Neil's conduct after the explosion. When we first meet Neil, he is in a sorry state, still suffering from shell shock. However, he apparently takes strength from the familiar surroundings of Halifax and from his reunion with Penny, for he is able to withstand the shock of being caught up in the Halifax disaster. After the explosion he organizes a clearing station for the wounded, and Angus Murray later remarks that Neil "had done excellent work, and few others had shown equal resourcefulness" (307). However, we must accept Murray's judgment on faith, just as we must elsewhere accept Penny's high assessment of Neil's ship-designing talents. The problem is that we actually see Neil do very little. The evidence for his remarkable intellect and for his leadership qualities comes from the statements of other people, not from Neil's deeds.

Perhaps Neil's strongest moment comes when he asserts his intention to resist Colonel Wain. He tells Angus Murray that he means to avoid the fate that befell his father:

"My father was born in a little village in Cape Breton—like yourself, I guess. He never had much schooling but the Bible. But he learned to build ships too, and he happened to be more than good. He might have been as good as [Donald] MacKay if he'd lived earlier. But hardly anyone heard of him, either. And when he died it wasn't in Nova Scotia. It was in Boston, where they've long ago forgotten how to breed seamen or build a ship. What I'm trying to say is . . . this province is my home."(178)

As he asserts his own identity, Neil expresses the fundamental theme of the novel: that a sense of identity can be achieved only by understanding and accepting one's past.

This theme applies to Neil at a symbolic as well as a personal level. In MacLennan's eyes, Neil is clearly a representative figure, the postcolonial Canadian. Neil's rebirth out of European violence represents a turning away from a civilization whose problems have grown insurmountable. Like Neil, Halifax itself learns to assert its identity in the face of adversity. Neil remarks to Penny: "This is a good town. . . . Professional soldiers could have been demoralized by a lot less than these people have taken" (320). MacLennan makes Neil the mouthpiece for his belief that the center of Western civilization lies in the newly awakened New World. And Canada, Neil reflects, will have a special role to play in transmitting the New World's healing influence:

Canada was still hesitant, was still ham-strung by men with the mentality of Geoffrey Wain. But if there were enough Canadians like himself, half-American and half-English, then the day was inevitable when the halves would join and his country would become the central arch which united the new order. (324-25)

Just as Neil is the book's hero, Penny Wain is its heroine. But, as with Neil, MacLennan has trouble showing us Penny's merits. When she is introduced, Penny is described as a woman of unusual talents. She works as a ship designer, and her plan for a submarine chaser has just been accepted by the British Admiralty. But Penny's apparent role as a feminist rebel is quickly undercut. It turns out that the ship's revolutionary design is really based on an idea casually mentioned one day by her cousin Neil. Penny's apparent self-sufficiency is also shown to be a facade, an effort to alleviate her inner emptiness:

Penny continued sitting at her desk, tense and solitary in the empty room. It was as though a stone had been plunged into the pool of her mind until her memories were surging like troubled waters, and for a few moments her whole body ached with loneliness and a sense of loss. The anaesthetic of hard work could never compensate for the feeling of life and growth that had departed from her. (23)

Penny's loneliness and sense of loss, we discover, are the result of the supposed death of Neil Macrae. The day before Neil embarked for Europe, he and Penny made love; Penny conceived a child who is now being raised by her Aunt Mary Fraser. By absorbing herself in her job at the shipyard, Penny has been "trying to outwit the Almighty by handing over her daughter to a kindly uncle and aunt, pretending that her sole ambition was to succeed in a man's profession" (216). The implication is clear: Penny's real ambition is to succeed in a woman's usual role as wife and mother. When Penny is reunited with Neil, she becomes a conventionally submissive female: "She was tied to this man, and the realization made her shiver. She was a prisoner of his maleness because once she had wanted him and he had refused to forget it" (318). As the novel concludes, Penny has regained her family. Yet her prospects for happiness seem dubious, for Neil's aptitude for domesticity seems slight.

MacLennan's deepest vision of Penny is as the girl in the garden (the first of several similar archetypal figures in his novels), not as the feminist ship designer. In her lonely reverie, Penny

> remembered things as they had been before the war. She saw herself dancing at an Admiralty House ball. She recollected the odor of lime trees heavy in the streets on close summer nights when there were shooting stars, and how those evenings as she walked alone it had been possible to imagine an aeon of tranquillity broadening out like a sea under the sky, herself growing old gently, with children about her, the land where she had been born mellowing slowly into maturity. (23)

MacLennan uses this prewar garden as he used Nova Scotia in his unpublished novels, as the image of a safe haven far removed from the troubled present. Always in MacLennan's fiction, there exists such a pastoral retreat, often a garden or a cottage in the country, which embodies the longing for escape to a simpler world felt by so many of his characters.

In Neil's absence, a rival contender for Penny's affections has appeared in Angus Murray, a doctor of medicine and a notorious drunk. Murray, like Edward Eisenhardt in "A Man Should Rejoice," is an eccentric older man, one of the many such figures in MacLennan's fiction who serve as counselors to the younger characters. Murray eventually helps Neil to secure the evidence he needs to vindicate himself, but first he lends piquancy to the opening portion of the novel by assuming the role of suitor to Penny. Murray is potentially a complex character, containing in undeveloped form some of the self-lacerating character traits MacLennan later explores in greater detail, particularly in *Each Man's Son*. When we first meet him, Murray is introduced as a habitual drinker, and he is described by Aunt Maria as "that man who used to ruin his practice with drink wherever he went" (38). Moreover, the narrator tells us, "In spite of his uniform Murray looked disreputable" (39).

Murray's self-destructive behavior is ascribed to the sudden death of his much-loved young wife. At first Murray thinks that Penny could end his loneliness. He asks her, "Penny—are you as lonely as I am?" (51). But when Murray recognizes Penny's love for Neil, he not only steps aside but has the generosity to take Neil's part in the quarrel with Colonel Wain. Murray's short-lived love for Penny apparently revives his better self. At first he is filled with self-pity and goes on a binge, but next morning he finds that "for the first time in many years a vision of the truth failed to make him afraid" (213). He has reached the bottom emotionally, and now he discovers there are still things to live for: "the beauty of the world remained and he found himself able to enjoy it; it stayed a constant in spite of all mankind's hideous attempts to master it" (214). Murray thus becomes the first of several MacLennan characters who joyfully accept the world despite its imperfections. Murray's new attitude ends his concern with external circumstances; instead, he turns inward: "above all, he wanted to think and to have time to recover the only thing he had left in the world, the sense of his own personality" (304).

MacLennan ascribes Murray's integrity, as well as his tendency to bouts of lonely melancholy, to his birth and upbringing among the Highland Scots of Cape Breton. But Murray's present outlook also owes much to his familiarity with the classics. The action of MacLennan's novel stresses the destruction wrought by modern technology, but Murray reminds readers of all that is good in Western civilization:

Plato's *Republic,* the *Nichomachaean Ethics,* Rashdall's *Theory of Good and Evil,* Horace and Catullus, Thucydides, Shakespeare and Milton—these and others crowded through his vision as he hung wearily over the arm of his chair, a man grown suddenly old, with the bar of hope broken in his brain. "I'm glad I know about them," he said to himself. "In spite of everything, I'm glad of that." (208)

In *Barometer Rising,* it is Murray who inherits the quietism of Michael Carmichael and David Culver, whereas Neil Macrae emerges from limbo to pit himself energetically against the world.

Neil's opponent is Colonel Wain, the most extreme villain MacLennan ever put into a novel (if we except Hitler, who is discussed in *Voices in Time*). However, Colonel Wain's villainy, like Neil's heroism, is more talked about than shown in action. Colonel Wain has always disliked Neil, whose father came from a different social class than did the colonel's family. Moreover, Colonel Wain feels "a commanding sense of insult when other people stretched out a hand towards something belonging to him" (98). Apparently he numbers his daughter among his possessions. Colonel Wain has vindictively accused Neil of disobedience in order to cover up his own incompetence. We are told he is power-hungry, a "megalomaniac" (172). But we do not see him try to exert power over anyone except Neil and Angus Murray.

Instead of showing Colonel Wain manipulating other people, MacLennan uses the colonel's illicit sex life as the principal means of blackening his character. The colonel's attraction to his mistress Evelyn is given a strong flavor of sadism:

> Whenever he made love to her he seemed to be studying the effect he produced, and she knew that the basis of his desire lay in the fact that her perfectly formed body was as diminutive as a miniature, that it was easy to hurt, and that he could goad it into the convulsions of a pleasure she could rarely control. (103)

The colonel's vision of the political future is just as shabby as his sex life. He believes that after the war "a new age would be at hand of power and vulgarity without limitation, in which the prizes would not be won by the qualified but by the cunning and unscrupulous" (189). Colonel Wain's vision of a world of "vulgarity and power" seems strange coming from someone of his background of colonial gentility. Nonetheless, MacLennan uses Colonel Wain to embody the modern power-hungry mentality. Although *Barometer Rising* is usually seen in a purely Canadian context as an expression of awakening national pride, MacLennan has in fact not forgotten the "international" concerns of his unpublished novels.

Elspeth Cameron points out that MacLennan viewed *Barometer Rising* as an antiwar novel.[4] The Halifax explosion is his symbol of the violence the Second World War was inflicting on European civilization even as he wrote. The explosion happened when a munitions ship, the *Mont Blanc*, collided with a relief ship, the *Imo*. To MacLennan, the result of this collision summarized the course of twentieth-century history: humanitarian impulses were everywhere falling victim to the forces of destruction. The explosion has several additional meanings. Its accidental nature reinforces one of the book's basic themes: the subordination of human affairs to the random course of events in the modern world. The explosion is also an image for the sudden accession of self-knowledge that violently catapults both Neil and Canada out of their somnolent states and into full self-awareness.

A major theme of MacLennan's fiction is the apparently arbitrary nature of events in the modern world. In *Barometer Rising,* this theme emerges most clearly from comments made by both narrator and characters. "Nothing matters in the world but chance," Jim Fraser tells his wife, only half in jest (190). Neil Macrae seeks to assert his identity despite feeling that "his world was composed now of nothing but chance" (12). Penny Wain recognizes that she has been caught "in the current of forces she had been able neither to predict nor control" (24). Angus Murray reflects, "The long failure of his life, the inability to alter the nature with which he had been born, had made him a fatalist against all his wishes" (50). Colonel Wain, the narrator tells us, was reduced to confused near-panic when his attack failed, and he realized "war was now neither a game nor a profession, but something he couldn't control or understand" (199–200). And Halifax itself, Murray tells us, "seemed governed by a fate she neither made nor understood" (50).

MacLennan's characters revolt against the sense of being controlled by external forces, and the novel concludes on a note of hope for the future. But in fact the novel's conflicts are resolved by yet another chance event: the Halifax explosion. The reunion between Neil and Penny is not a logical resolution of the issues MacLennan's story has posed. The novel asks whether humanity has any power in the face of the momentum of man's own technological creations. Penny expresses this dilemma when she says of Neil, "By nature he would fight indefinitely to achieve a human significance in an age where the products of human ingenuity made mockery of the men who had created them" (321). She adds the hope that Neil may "gain his significance, just as within the last few days he had achieved his dignity" (321). But Neil himself reflects at the novel's end, "For better or worse he was entering the future, he was identifying himself with the still-hidden forces which were doomed to shape humanity as certainly as the tiny states of Europe had shaped the past" (324).

MacLennan's only solution to the dilemma of individual powerlessness has a desperate ring to it. Like Angus Murray, Penny Wain recognizes the necessity to commit herself to an unknown future:

> She was in the current now. She had been in it ever since that night in Montreal, except that by synthetic action she had tried to pretend she was safe on dry land, safe with the accumulated weight of her environment to support her. She could see nothing clearly ahead. To force one's self on into the darkness, to keep one's integrity as one moved—this was all that mattered because this was all there was left. (320)

Penny's thoughts here anticipate the attitude of George Stewart, who also comes to accept that he is adrift in a current he cannot control. But in *Barometer Rising,* the notion that one can only exercise control over one's inner self is not the main theme. Instead, MacLennan evades the determinism that seems implicit in his plot by ending the novel with the reunion of the lovers. This conclusion seems to reflect a bit of wish fulfillment on MacLennan's part, for the happy ending is given to characters whose lives have hitherto moved along a rigorously determined path.

On the surface, *Barometer Rising* seems to end with the resolution of all conflicts. The lovers are reunited and regain their daughter. The nation emerges from its bondage to a colonial outlook. However, a careful reading shows that important issues remain unresolved at the end of the novel. The characters are still in the grip of social and technological forces they cannot control. Moreover, although the book ends with the reunion of lovers, its presentation of sexuality is actually highly ambivalent. In the novel's scheme of punishments and rewards, Neil and Penny have paid a high price for their mutual attraction. Neil has nearly been killed on a European battlefield, and Penny has almost been blinded by a flying splinter of glass. Colonel Wain pays an even higher price for his sexual indulgence, for he is found dead beside his mistress.

Perhaps the greatest omission of all is the book's failure to acknowledge the strength of the hostility between Neil and Colonel Wain. In effect, the plot of *Barometer Rising* splits Neil's father into two figures. The biological father is portrayed as wholly admirable; but he dies offstage, so that Neil is raised in the home of a repellent foster-father onto whom is projected all the hostility a child might sometimes feel toward his real father. MacLennan's plot therefore disguises a father-son conflict as a conventional struggle between hero and villain. Neil is not the literal agent of Colonel Wain's death, but the convenience of the death is too neat to be passed off as mere chance. The novel's plot is dreaming on Neil's behalf. The psychological action of the novel is a gradual revelation of the tensions by acting out the logical outcome of Neil's hostility to Colonel Wain without openly attributing that hostility to Neil.

Colonel Wain's death clears the way for Neil's reunion with Penny. There is an incestuous overtone to this romance, for Penny is Neil's cousin, and she and Neil have been raised as brother and sister. Moreover, an incestuous aura hovers over Angus Murray's fondness for Penny. Murray is of the colonel's generation; he is not a contemporary of Neil. At one point, the colonel even suggests that he will encourage Murray's romance with Penny if Murray cooperates in eliminating Neil. Therefore, the short-lived attraction between Murray and Penny has more than a hint of a father-daughter relationship, and the rivalry between Murray and Neil is an oedipal rivalry in disguise. The book's action never forces Neil and Penny to face up to the real basis of their attraction. By keeping their affections within the family, Neil and Penny may simply be refusing to grow up.

The only expression of the oedipal tensions that underlie the novel takes place indirectly, though dramatically, through the explosion that devastates so much of Halifax. The explosion is logically a deus ex machina, but it has a coherent place in the novel's psychological development. The explosion's violence is an image of the potentially overwhelming power of the sexual impulse to overcome human reason and induce destructively uncontrolled behavior. In relation to Neil, the explosion functions as an extended primal scene, a magnified image of the child's fearful misunderstanding of the nature of parental sexuality.

Among the victims of the explosion are Colonel Wain and his mistress—and Evelyn, incidentally, is about the same age as Penny. Surely it is not coincidence that Neil should be the one to find their bodies in circumstances that clearly indicate the sexual nature of their relationship. First Neil sees "a girl's body, entirely naked and exposed." Then:

> As he was trying to find a foothold to climb back, a plank broke loose and the man's face was revealed. Neil stood staring as the beam of the torch fell on the frozen, familiar features of Geoffrey Wain. His fingers slipped on the switch and he was in darkness, his knees shaking and the tired blood throbbing through his temples. (302)

Consider what these images imply. Neil has discovered his stepfather's sexuality at the same time as he discovers the colonel's death. That is, the death seems to come as punishment for the sexuality of the father-figure. These psychological undercurrents are not made explicit and may not be apparent to most casual readers. Nonetheless, they help the novel to achieve its undeniable power.

The novel's action also reflects tensions that were present in MacLennan himself at the time he wrote it. He was still young; he still had his way to make in the world. He refused to accept the failure of his two novels as a final judgment on his literary talent. In a symbolic act of self-assertion, he created a protagonist whose outlook is both materialistic and scientific. Neil Macrae is a man of action rather than thought, a hero who triumphs over the repressive old order. At this time, the death of Dr. Sam was still fresh in his mind. To criticize his father directly remained unthinkable.

Yet, just as he projected his own determination to succeed onto Neil Macrae, MacLennan also projected his hostility toward Dr. Sam into the story of Geoffrey Wain's death. By killing Colonel Wain in the Halifax explosion, MacLennan was able to conceal—perhaps even from himself—the true nature of the emotions that prompted his story. The book achieved a public success, which helped to satisfy MacLennan's need for recognition; but the book's emotional evasions demonstrate that at this time MacLennan's private journey was still in its early stages.

Two Solitudes

In *Barometer Rising,* MacLennan celebrated his discovery of Canada as a political entity. But in that novel he portrayed a very limited world, the upper-middle-class society of Halifax. True, he made Neil think of Canada as the "central arch" that would link Great Britain with the United States. But this was really a gross oversimplification; he was portraying the country as though it were a single homogeneous unit. MacLennan really knew better. In Montreal he had learned to see Canada as a political compromise based on the uneasy alliance of two quite different peoples. This was the political vision that he would embody in his next novel.

The generally favorable response to *Barometer Rising* had certainly heartened MacLennan, though there is a tone of regret in his comment, made in a letter to his friend George Barrett, that he was now "doomed to continue" in the use of Canadian settings. But the enthusiastic Canadian response to the novel had given MacLennan "the certain knowledge that Canadians are hungry for a spokesman."[5] With some deliberateness, MacLennan set out to make himself that spokesman.

In *Two Solitudes* he tried to distill the essence of the Canadian experience by showing how the tensions in Canadian society influenced one boy's troubled growth to manhood. If his plan succeeded, he proclaimed to Barrett in another letter, he would "at least solve the dilemma of how to handle a Canadian novel." In writing *Barometer Rising,* MacLennan had felt restricted by "the deliberate limitations I imposed on myself for the sake of the market."[6] Now, the success of his novel bolstered his self-confidence, and he felt free to pursue his preference for a more expansive kind of fiction. In *Two Solitudes* his model would be the "novel of scope," such as a book he had recently read by the German writer Jakob Wasserman, *The World's Illusion,*[7] or the family sagas written by his perennial favorite Galsworthy, or the encyclopedic surveys produced by that deity among novelists, Tolstoy.

Like *Barometer Rising*, *Two Solitudes* is a variant on the historical romance. The fate of particular individuals is played out against a background of events that are molding the course of twentieth-century history. But the two books have different emphases, which can be illustrated by comparing their openings. The first pages of *Barometer Rising* follow the actions and thoughts of a particular character, the returned soldier Neil Macrae. But in the first pages of *Two Solitudes*, a historical lecture is blended with a scenic tour narrated by an all-seeing observer suspended somewhere high over the St. Lawrence valley. In short, *Barometer Rising* focuses on the fate of a few individuals, whereas *Two Solitudes* sets out to tell a story about two large social groups.

Two Solitudes is very much a novel with a message. MacLennan wants to urge Canadians of both founding races to reconcile their differences. In the St. Lawrence valley, the narrator says, "Two old races and religions meet . . . and live their separate legends, side by side" (4). The French Catholic legend is communal and conservative, and presents French-Canadians as a race of farmers bound in sacred trust to the soil and to their religion as in Louis Hémon's *Maria Chapdelaine*. The English Protestant legend is quite different, for the English way of life has no larger collective purpose. The English live as individuals, each pursuing private goals: "The production, acquisition and distribution of wealth was about the only purpose they ever seemed able to find" (88). Athanase Tallard becomes the spokesman for MacLennan's discontent with Canadians of both races when he says to Yardley:

"This country is so new that when you see it for the first time, all of it, and particularly the west, you feel like Columbus and you say to yourself, 'My God, is all this ours!' Then you make the trip back. You come across Ontario and you encounter the mind of the maiden aunt. You see the Methodists in Toronto and the Presbyterians in the best streets of Montreal and the Catholics all over Quebec, and nobody understands one damn thing except that he's better than everyone else. The French are Frencher than France and the English are more British than England ever dared to be. And then you go to Ottawa and you see the Prime Minister with his ear to the ground and his backside hoisted in the air. And, Captain Yardley, you say God damn it!" (28)

The action of Part 1 is smoothly constructed to highlight the main features of Canada's dual heritage. Captain Yardley's purchase of the Dansereau farm calls forth the historical French-Canadian antogonism toward the English, based largely on ignorance and buttressed by the

Church's antiassimilationist policy. The conflict between Athanase and Father Beaubien embodies the traditional tension within Quebec society between unquestioning faith and a more skeptical, even anticlerical outlook. Huntly McQueen's plan to build a factory in Saint-Marc introduces the conflict between the traditional agricultural way of life and a rapidly industrializing economy. All this takes place against a background of heightened French-English tensions created by the war, when the English majority imposed conscription on the French, many of whom saw no reason to defend either the France that had once deserted them or the England that had conquered them.

Two Solitudes is constructed on an altogether more generous scale than is *Barometer Rising*. The characterizations are both more numerous and more varied; and more of the characters seem worth the reader's sympathy or dislike. Athanase is appealing, despite his self-centered nature; Yardley is a thoroughly engaging eccentric; Janet Methuen is eminently disagreeable; and Huntly McQueen is a fascinating study of a sometimes repellent character. Perhaps Marius is a bit too much of a stereotype, and Daphne Methuen too transparently a sexual adventuress; but MacLennan's secondary characters are usually portrayed in sufficient detail to give his story a richly varied surface of incident and personality. Of the major characters, only Paul Tallard and Heather Methuen, when they take over as central figures of the novel's second portion, do not seem adequately imagined. They become too obviously the vehicle for expressing MacLennan's message.

Captain Yardley is the novel's best example of a freely invented character who has no transparently obvious didactic purpose. He is exuberantly eccentric in speech and behavior, and thoroughly kindhearted. If he has a specific purpose in the novel, aside from allowing MacLennan to introduce a few digressions on Nova Scotia, it is to act as a warmly indulgent and approving surrogate parent to Paul. Soon after moving to Saint-Marc, Yardley realizes that "he had come to love young Paul as though the boy were his own son" (61). Paul notices that, unlike Athanase who never listens carefully to his son, "Captain Yardley always listened to him, and then talked about what he'd said as though it mattered" (83).

But it is Athanase who is the novel's most complex and most subtly imagined character. Pride and independence are the keynotes of his personality. He tries to apply Gallic rationality to his life and is "intolerant of authority unless it was the authority of the mind, of the logical idea" (126). His independence of mind sometimes overwhelms his good judgment. He takes a proconscription stand because he will not let either tradition or the Church dictate his thinking. Yet his unpopular political views do not help to promote national unity and only do him personal harm. Athanase's private difficulties involve both Kathleen, his young wife, and Marius, his discontented older son. Athanase embarks on his disastrous business venture at least partly because he wants to regain his self-confidence, bruised by the failure of his parliamentary career, and because he wishes to present himself to Kathleen as an active and successful figure. However, when he agrees to start a factory in Saint-Marc, Athanase begins the course of action that eventually strands him between two worlds.

Athanase's story is the tragedy of a man who loses his place in his own society and discovers that he has also lost his identity, which had been conferred on him by his membership in that society. Athanase wants to assist the entry of Quebec into the new world of science and technology. But in the end he only alienates himself from Quebec. In childish anger, he then leaves Saint-Marc and declares himself a Presbyterian! But he discovers that the English, who run the technological world, do not want him either. He discovers that though he cannot live within his community, neither can he live without its support. As he weakens and lies dying, his mind projects images from his Catholic past. When he dies, Marius smugly proclaims that Athanase's apparent last-minute return to the Church is a miracle. This concern for Athanase's spiritual welfare is ironic, coming from the person who, above all others—even more than McQueen—destroys him.

The antipathy Marius feels toward Athanase is sexual in origin. Marius overheard Athanase making love to Kathleen on the very evening his first wife died. To Athanase, this encounter was an affirmation of his commitment to life, but to Marius, it was a desecration of the memory of his saintlike mother. Marius admires his mother for her devotion and for her ascetic way of life. He views her as an ideal Catholic. His bitterness at others really expresses his dissatisfaction with himself, because he can never measure up to his image of his mother's perfection. He not only experiences sexual feelings, which he has been taught to regard as sinful, but he is also strongly drawn to his stepmother, Kathleen, whom he feels he ought to hate.

Kathleen, with her sensuous grace, exerts the fascination of the forbidden. Marius has tried to adhere to an overly rigid and restrictive moral outlook, and as a result his natural impulses are frustrated. Marius is unknowingly controlled by his thwarted sexuality. He marries Emilie because she embodies his theoretical ideal of French-Canadian womanhood, but she can never meet his real needs. Marius's rabidly nationalistic politics are an outlet for both his frustrated sexual energy and his self-reproach, neither of which he can express directly.

It is Marius who triggers the reversal in Athanase's fortunes, by giving Father Beaubien damaging information to use in blackening Athanase's reputation in the parish. More importantly, the long-delayed revelation that Marius knows of his father's misdeed causes Athanase virtually to collapse. The orthodox-minded Marius has always been unable to accept his father's conduct, and now Athanase finds that part of his own mind also reproaches him for what he did with Kathleen. When Father Beaubien accuses him, Athanase is overcome by "the sense of guilt aroused in him" (148). It is no good telling himself that by loving Kathleen "he had swum upward out of death" (149). He discovers that he cannot wholly free himself from the moral standards of the Church.

The relationship between Marius and Athanase is a father-son conflict that is so intense it can only end destructively. The force of Marius's emotion is emphasized by the strategy of concealing both the nature of Athanase's deed and Marius's knowledge about his father until the moment when Beaubien confronts Athanase. By delaying the disclosure of Athanase's conduct, MacLennan arranges to juxtapose a primal scene with a father's downfall, just as he also does near the end of *Barometer Rising*.

MacLennan's novel contains another striking scene in which sexuality is prominent. This is the encounter between Kathleen and Dennis Morey. Readers familiar with contemporary fiction, in which the most intimate details of the sexual act are commonplace, may be surprised to learn that when *Two Solitudes* was published, such scenes provoked criticism. Indeed, Penny's illegitimate child and Colonel Wain's mistress had previously drawn down a certain amount of moral wrath on *Barometer Rising*. Respectable Canadians, many people felt, just did not behave in this way. When *Two Solitudes* was published, several reviewers attacked the book for its immorality. And among the letters MacLennan received was one that trumpeted: "I want to ask you what kind of moral pervert you are . . . that you cannot see even one single woman without concentrating on her thighs and breasts?"[8]

Despite a narrow outlook, the letter writer has a point: MacLennan does explain his characters' motives almost wholly in sexual terms. Athanase has always needed women to sustain his sense of self-worth. Marius feels a strong attraction to Kathleen, and much of his conduct is the expression of redirected sexual energies. Huntly McQueen puts into his work all the energies that a normal man might divide between his work and his family. Janet Methuen's self-control mirrors her frigidity. At one point, Daphne's husband Noel Fletcher makes a pass at Heather, and we learn that for him sex is more a contest of wills than an expression of tender emotions. Throughout the book, sexuality is mingled into the characters' motives. As Daphne says to Heather, "Sex is much more devious than simply going to bed with a man" (255). Only Heather and Paul appear to experience a normal sexuality. The disturbed sexuality in most of the other characters reflects MacLennan's belief that unbalanced sexual conduct is frequently a symptom of a deeper psychological imbalance.

But MacLennan does not portray sexuality in itself as a negative force. Consider the occasion when Kathleen and Dennis Morey end their evening by making love. Superficially, Kathleen is simply an adulteress. But she feels "that this had happened in accordance with some deep necessity" (117). Kathleen and Morey help each other to recover a sense of self-worth; they rekindle each other's joy in simply being alive. Kathleen is not a selfish sensualist, but someone who needs to use her one talent, "to be herself: easy, natural, giving and accepting without question, never thinking beyond the moment" (109). The "deep necessity" Kathleen feels is simply a need not to do violence to her essential inner self. The scene echoes the previous life-renewing encounter between Kathleen and Athanase, but this time it is Kathleen who is revived. The scene also anticipates the encounter of Jerome Martell and Catherine Carey in *The Watch That Ends the Night*. Dennis Morey has a vitality that matches Jerome's. Like Jerome, he is spontaneous and unwilling to conform to conventional standards when he regards those standards as hypocritical. However, the scene between Kathleen and Dennis is intrusive in *Two Solitudes*, for Dennis Morey meets Kathleen once and then just disappears from the novel.

Before Morey vanishes, however, MacLennan does make him the spokesman for a political message. Morey tells Kathleen that Canadians are all "puritans." They repress their natural instincts and call that repression virtue. Canadians are safe, honest, reliable—and dull. Morey asks, "Why do people hate beauty in this country the way they do?" (114). And he complains that Montreal imitates "every example of bad taste in the universe" (114). But MacLennan's extensive investigation of Canadian "puritanism" really begins in his next novel, *The Precipice*. In *Two Solitudes*, Morey's ideas are secondary to another political question, the division between French and English.

The title of MacLennan's novel has given Canadians a catch phrase to describe their country's split personality. MacLennan took the phrase from a passage in a letter by the German poet Rainer Maria Rilke that appeals to the power of love to heal the separateness of individuals: "Love consists in this, that two solitudes protect, and touch, and greet each other." MacLennan wanted the passage, which he used as the book's epigraph, to apply to the love story of Paul Tallard and Heather Methuen, who reach across the boundary between the nation's two founding cultural groups. Nonetheless, readers have persistently read the title primarily in relation to the division between French and English communities.

MacLennan has only himself to blame if his title has been misinterpreted. He began by planning a book that would follow the shaping of a representative Canadian artist, Paul Tallard.[9] However, this young artist needed a father, so MacLennan imagined Athanase Tallard. Before long, the aging seigneur had taken over the first portion of the novel, which swelled to half the book's final length. MacLennan enlarged Athanase's role because this was a convenient way of introducing a great deal of information about Quebec's history and present society. Without this information, he felt the story would lack an explanatory foundation. But in addition, the emergence of Athanase as the book's most appealing and most fully rendered character is further evidence of MacLennan's fascination with fathers, and evidence of his interest in the acute hostility that can exist within the family.

The importance of Athanase's role has given the novel a conspicuous structural weakness. *Two Solitudes* falls into two sharply divided sections. Part 1 and Part 2 combine to form a masterful exposition of the causes behind the decline of Athanase Tallard. In this portion of the novel, the characters are integral parts of their social backgrounds and the conflicts flow naturally out of the interaction of personality with social factors. The seamless union of personal and public dimensions makes this portion of *Two Solitudes* one of the high points of MacLennan's fiction. But in Part 3 and Part 4, MacLennan tells the story of Athanase's youngest son, Paul, who was merely a rather passive observer of the events in the novel's first portion. The episodic action of Parts 3 and 4 is spread thinly over a span of six years; and Paul's story tries, without complete success, to encompass an almost impossible variety of themes.

Paul is less complex than his father. He is thwarted not by his French-Canadian background but by the Depression. He becomes a representative figure, someone who remembers "doors closing in his face, the regretful smiles of older, well-established men; the knowledge eating into himself and millions of others month by month and year by year that nobody wanted them, nobody could find a use for them" (252). Paul comes into conflict with such representatives of the older generation as Janet Methuen and Huntly McQueen; but he has no philosophy or viewpoint of his own to offer in place of theirs, except perhaps a vaguely expressed faith in the scientific outlook that is sweeping Western civilization. Paul is not one of MacLennan's typically guilt-haunted young men. And precisely because he carries no private torment within himself, Paul is less alive inwardly than even the young men protrayed in MacLennan's unpublished novels.

Heather is presented as the nonconforming member of the Methuen family, refusing marriage to a safe member of the Montreal establishment and aspiring to become a painter. Although she knows the world is full of economic misery, she has not succumbed to either gloom or cynicism. Paul tells her: "You're a happy person. You've got joy inside you. For God's sake don't be ashamed of it. The world is dying for the lack of it" (277). Despite the joyless people who surround her, Heather continues to seek "the fire she knew was still alive in the world, somewhere, if she could find it" (256). She is another one of MacLennan's girls in the garden. Although she is not, like Penny Wain, associated with the odor of lime trees, she does appear dressed in "lime green" (230), as is Catherine Carey in a later novel. And Paul tells Heather, "I'd like to see you cutting roses in the garden" (332). Like Penny Wain, Heather apparently abandons her personal ambitions once she has been united with her soul mate: "She loved him so utterly he had become her way of life. For a man it could never be the same. He had his work, he had the ruthless drive inside that would never let him alone" (321).

Paul and Heather are often treated as symbols rather than individuals. Their marriage is meant to point the way to a reconciliation of French and English. Yardley decides "that each was the victim of the two racial legends within the country." He reflects:

On both sides, French and English, the older generation was trying to freeze the country and make it static. . . . Yet the country was changing. In spite of them all it was drawing together; but in a personal, individual way, and slowly, French and English getting to know each other as individuals in spite of the rival legends. (270)

But this meaning seems to be forced onto the story. Paul and Heather—Paul especially—seem to have already freed themselves of social and familial ties when the novel's second portion begins.

MacLennan projected many aspects of his own life into the story of Heather and Paul. Their marriage is hindered by Paul's economic problems, as MacLennan felt his career had been hindered and his marriage delayed by the Depression. Paul's efforts to become a writer resemble MacLennan's own efforts during the thirties. In Huntly McQueen and Janet Methuen, MacLennan creates parental figures who seem bent on denying emotional and physical fulfillment to the younger generation. In contrast, Captain Yardley is an idealized father figure, who approves of the marriage and supports Paul's literary ambitions. "This country's going to be mighty proud of thet boy one of these days" (311), Yardley tells Janet.

The story of Paul's efforts to become a writer reaches its climax with his decision to write about his own country. Paul's attempt to create an international novel has led him to a dead end. As Heather tells him: "Your characters are all naturally vital people. But your main theme never gives them a chance. It keeps asserting that they're doomed" (328). Why Paul's decision to write about Canada should resolve this dilemma is not clear. Apparently, he feels that unspoiled Canadian vitality and innocence can triumph where European decadence has failed. However flimsy the logic here, the result is that *Two Solitudes* tacitly asserts what *Barometer Rising* openly proclaimed: that Canada would play a leading part in creating a new society free of the burden of European failures.

Paul's decision does represent an acceptance of himself as a Canadian and indicates that he retains faith in himself. Like Neil Macrae, Paul is an active hero, even if his heroic action consists only of writing a book. He does not use his art to turn away from the world of everyday experience as David Culver did, but plans to put the experiential world into his novel. Paul is therefore not a Joycean artist—at least not as MacLennan understands Joyce. Paul's book will aim not at manipulating styles and symbols in order to create an esthetically pleasing effect but at re-creating experience. Nor is Paul a disciple of Hemingway. He will use his art not to celebrate the superiority of his private experience but to forge a renewed link between himself and his society.

Paul's brother Marius is an example of the course Paul has wisely avoided. Marius is now a failed lawyer and a failed politican; he spends his time plotting futilely to start his own political party. When Paul visits Marius, he realizes, "With every sentence he uttered, Marius was binding the strait-jacket tighter and tighter around himself" (337). After the visit, Paul concludes: "In seeing Marius he had seen more than his brother; he had seen the symbol of much of his past frustration" (338). To underline the contrast between the brothers, MacLennan follows Paul's visit to Marius with a contrasting scene:

> Instead of going home he [Paul] kept on walking till past midnight, when he stopped at a Murray's for coffee and a sandwich. He listened to the talk of night-workers around him. They were relaxed and easy with each other, French and English together, radio technicians, theatre operators, telegraphers, men who had walked up from the railroad stations. None of them seemed worried or strained. They were together because of the nature of their jobs, and because the rest of the city was asleep. (338)

Although these men belong to two races, they are bound in common fealty to the machine. They symbolize the nation's future. But here MacLennan has created a difficulty. To align Paul with a scientific outlook is to align him with Daphne's arrogant husband, the ruthless Noel Fletcher, and with the industrialist Huntly McQueen. Indeed, science is the all-powerful force shaping the mechanized world Paul fearfully depicts in his novel "Young Men of 1933." At the end of *Two Solitudes,* Canada is "alone with history, with science, with the future" (370). This does not sound reassuring. And at the novel's end, Paul plans to enlist in the armed forces. This plan seems to make him the victim rather than the master of the destructive forces threatening society.

The character whose story reaches the most satisfactory conclusion is Captain Yardley. At his death, Yardley, unlike Athanase and indeed unlike anyone else in the novel, has made peace with himself and with the world. He knows there is an "ultimate solitude" surrounding the human condition; and he is "persuaded that all knowledge is like a painted curtain hung across the door of the mind to conceal from it a mystery so darkly suggestive that no one can face it alone for long" (61). In his memory of "sharks and barracuda [moving] in their three-dimensional element, self-centred, beautiful, dangerous and completely aimless" (61), Yardley finds an apt image of the inscrutable universe, whose purposes man cannot fathom. Yet his death is unlike Athanase's embittered end. Yardley has the inner resources to face an indifferent world with equanimity. In his last days, "it seemed to Yardley that with the talent and the courage there was no limit to what a man could obtain out of life if he merely accepted what lay all around him" (316). This note of resignation, reminiscent of David Culver in "A Man Should Rejoice," does not occur again in MacLennan's work until it becomes the keynote of *The Watch That Ends the Night.*

There is a certain incompleteness to both of MacLennan's national romances. At the end of *Barometer Rising,* Neil Macrae faces a world on the verge of dramatic change, a world in which science will be the dominant force. In *Two Solitudes,* Paul faces a world just embarked on total war, a world threatened by the fiery violence unleashed by science. In both books, the protagonist becomes a believer in a materialistic outlook and prepares to join a society in which science and technology will provide the dominant values. Both novels deal with a Canadian society on the verge of transformation. The reader may well ask: What will happen to Canada in the new scientific era that Neil and Paul foresee? MacLennan's novels do not provide an answer to this question.

In *Barometer Rising* and *Two Solitudes,* MacLennan tries to resolve social and political problems by dissolving them in an outburst of emotion. The lovers declare their independence from repressive parental figures; youth, energy, and new ideas appear to be victorious over the restrictive old order. But in his next novel MacLennan starts where *Barometer Rising* and *Two Solitudes* leave off. He begins with a love story and follows it into marriage; he also follows Canada's fortunes through the war years and into the postwar era.

Chapter Four
The Calvinist Legacy

In a 1946 article, MacLennan announced the view of Canada to which he has adhered throughout his career. He described the country as based on an unlikely alliance of three superficially dissimilar peoples: French Canadians, United Empire Loyalists, and Highland Scots:

> As different from one another as these groups may be by nature, they share a common psychological inheritance. Because they all became Canadians as a result of finding themselves on the losing side in war and politics, they are all cautious, conservative, and suspicious of change. They are intensely loyal by nature, to the group as well as to the King of England. Even the French-Canadians honor the King. Taking a natural part in North American progress, they still tend to distrust it, casting an eye back to the symbols of the old countries which have been handed down faithfully from father to son.[1]

These conclusions provided a basis for MacLennan's belief that Canada was different from such a wholly progress-obsessed nation as the United States.

The article also expressed an idea that provided MacLennan with the impetus for the next stage of his career. He now saw the most important distinguishing feature of Canadian society as a conservatism that had survived long after such attitudes had vanished in the United States. However, Canadian conservatism—which MacLennan closely identified with a Calvinist or puritan outlook—was now "threatened with exactly the same kind of revolt we have witnessed in the United States." And he proclaimed, "Here is perhaps the most important theme for a Canadian writer today." As he wrote his next two novels, *The Precipice* and *Each Man's Son,* MacLennan carried out his analysis of Canadian puritanism. In *The Precipice,* he compares Canadian and American variants of the Calvinist legacy; in *Each Man's Son,* he studies the Calvinism that existed among the Protestant Highland Scots who settled in Nova Scotia.

The Precipice

By many readers, *The Precipice* has been nominated as MacLennan's worst novel. Critics complain that the plot is sentimental to the point of cliché, that many of the characters are little more than stereotypes, that the second half of the book is clumsily constructed, and that the narrative technique is often intrusively didactic. Nonetheless, MacLennan's third novel does contain some interesting scenes and characters, and perhaps more importantly, it marks a significant shift in the direction of MacLennan's career.

The Precipice tells the story of the ill-fated romance of Lucy Cameron and Stephen Lassiter. However, the crucial force shaping events in the novel is not the attraction between the two lovers but the attitudes implanted in them by their fathers and their societies. The romance is heavily shadowed by an almost irresistible working out of parental influences, which in turn were shaped by closely related versions of the outlook MacLennan likes to describe as "puritan." Thus, MacLennan's love story leads him to a discussion of the lingering effects of Calvinism on members of his own generation. Consequently, he is eventually forced to reconsider his entire attitude toward religion. And in the course of this reconsideration, MacLennan uncovers a reservoir of deeply divided feelings, which find expression in his subsequent fiction.

In the later stages of his career, MacLennan has shied away from what he sees as the dangers inherent in a materialistic outlook and has proposed a recognition, even a celebration, of the spiritual aspects of the human condition. This shift in outlook is first clearly announced in *The Precipice,* so that despite its weaknesses the book is a pivotal work in the MacLennan canon. The unresolved tensions in *The Precipice* are omens of the novels to follow. By exposing the repressive effects of strict Calvinism, MacLennan lays the groundwork for *Each Man's Son.* By concluding on an affirmative religious note, he announces the theme that will dominate *The Watch That Ends the Night* and will play a prominent part in *Return of the Sphinx.* In turning to a religious position, MacLennan—like his later fictional creation, George Stewart—has to question some of the political and economic ideas that have hitherto played a large part in his thought.

In *The Precipice,* MacLennan for the first time explicitly acknowledges one of his deepest preoccupations as a novelist. That preoccupation is failure—but failure of a particular kind: failure of nerve, failure of ambition and initiative, lack of self-confidence. MacLennan's eventual recognition of failure as a significant theme is foreshadowed in the two unpublished novels, and even in *Barometer Rising* and *Two Solitudes,* which contain troubled characters—namely Angus Murray and Athanase Tallard—who are more complex and interesting than the young men MacLennan casts as his major figures. In *The Precipice,* MacLennan deliberately creates a figure with an introverted, self-abasing personality—the chronic loser, Bruce Fraser.

The creation of Bruce Fraser is important, because he is so clearly a forerunner of George Stewart, the narrator and central figure of MacLennan's best novel, *The Watch That Ends the Night.* MacLennan uses Bruce, along with the American Stephen Lassiter, to highlight differences between Canadian and American attitudes to success and failure. Where Stephen pursues success to the exclusion of all else, Bruce retreats from life—he has failed before he even starts. However, Stephen ultimately turns out to be another version of the motif of self-induced failure. In fact, Bruce and Stephen are brothers under the skin, for MacLennan traces the principal features of both personalities to the lingering effects of a strongly Calvinist religious heritage.

The contrast between Bruce and Stephen is an important part of the design of *The Precipice.* Lucy decides: "Stephen Lassiter and Bruce Fraser could meet anywhere and know instinctively they were on opposite sides of whatever there was to be on opposite sides of. They were on opposite sides as human beings."[2] Bruce is an intellectual and a poet. At the outset of the novel, he thinks that "ideas were more important than people" (3), and he tries to fit historical events into grand theoretical patterns. Stephen Lassiter takes a pragmatic attitude toward the world: "He had none of Bruce Fraser's desire to make the world a better place. Almost, his conscious attitude seemed to state without words, 'I didn't make the rules. And I know, as in your heart you know, that there's nothing to be done about them'" (136). Stephen tries to extend the engineer's hardheaded preoccupation with "facts" into every aspect of his life. To a superficial observer, Stephen would seem to have uncritically assimilated the values of the commercial society in which he lives. Unlike Bruce, he seems to have no personal code which could set him at odds with society. Stephen's eventual downfall illustrates the pitfalls attendant on the pursuit of unlimited success. Bruce's story, on the other hand, enables MacLennan to examine what he perceives as a Canadian reluctance to even attempt success.

MacLennan has explained that his intention in *The Precipice* was "to find a common denominator between U.S. and Canadian tradition which I believe exists in the Puritan background of both countries."[3] In *The*

Precipice, Bruce Fraser and Lucy Cameron are beset by the same dilemma that is later examined in depth in *Each Man's Son.* Dr. Ainslie lucidly outlines the problem into which his father's teachings have led him: "The old Calvinist had preached that life was a constant struggle against evil, and his son had believed him. At the same time he had preached that failure was a sin. Now the man who had been the boy must ask, how could a successful man be sinless, or a sinless man successful?"[4] Stephen Lassiter confronts a secular version of this same dilemma. As Carl Bratian explains to Lucy: "Steve was trained to feel like a heel if he didn't make money and he was trained to feel like a heel if he made it the way everyone else makes it. So he's right in there between two sides of himself and he can't make up his mind to choose one or the other" (284). The stories of Stephen and Bruce, then, are simply two national variations on the pursuit of success—and also two studies in the failure of that quest.

Success and failure obsess most of the characters in *The Precipice.* When the reader first meets Bruce Fraser, Bruce is deep in self-pity, trying to excuse himself for "being unsuccessful at twenty-four" (4). Subsequently we learn that Bruce "had been a candidate for a Rhodes Scholarship and his failure to win it had been a bitter blow to his father" (45). Stephen Lassiter, despite his contempt for the advertising business, joins Carl Bratian's agency in New York, which he describes as "the city, where, no matter how many people pretended otherwise, the really successful men chose to live" (86). When her marriage to Stephen begins to deteriorate, Lucy tries to assess her life: "So she had failed. But had she? For a while at least she had lived. Had any woman failed if she had two happy children?" (296). In inverted form, the question of success or failure dominates the life of that splendid example of militant failure, Matt McCunn: "So long as there were people anywhere who rejected the idea of success, he was with them" (236).

The most spectacular failure examined in *The Precipice* is the bankruptcy of the American dream. Material success has failed to bring happiness to its devotees, Stephen Lassiter and Carl Bratian. These two men actually represent different stages in the development of the American dream. Stephen once trained as an engineer; he is still infatuated with technology and would like nothing better than to resume his involvement with machinery or even to become an inventor. Appropriately, Stephen first appears as an imported "efficiency expert" sent by the parent American firm to shape up the newly acquired Canadian subsidiary. Bratian's manipulation of Stephen shows how the essentially naive stage of fascination with technology has been superseded by the cynical exploitation of other people. Advertising has become more important to society than manufacturing; human engineering has replaced mechanical engineering as the quickest route to power and wealth.

As an efficiency expert, Stephen had been able to keep up a pretense to himself that he was acting as a kind of engineer. Moreover, he could retain some scope to exercise compassion for other people. There is a rumor in Grenville that Stephen's "recommendations had been more favorable to old Grenville employees than the parent company desired" (157). Even this vestige of humanity is denied to Stephen in Bratian's advertising agency. Bratian states the agency's philosophy with chilling directness:

> "The bigger the country gets, the less sure of himself every individual in it is going to become. All right. Go hard for nationalism. Go hard for sex. Go hard for efficiency. Make every grass-root in Kansas think it's getting a raw deal if it can't pass for an orchid. Keep on telling them they deserve the best because they're Americans and that the American way of life is the best because it's the most efficient. But don't forget this—the only thing *all* of them are interested in is sex. Think about it. Dream about it and you can't lose." (244).

As Lucy vainly tries to tell Stephen, "there's death in a man like Carl. Ultimately he kills whatever he touches. And the worst thing about him is that he knows exactly what he's doing" (275). Indeed, Carl does know what he's doing. He uses Stephen's technological aptitude to service the Harper Aircraft account during the war, but drops Stephen the moment the war ends and bombers are no longer a salable commodity.

Bratian contributes an important dimension to the analysis of American society, for he is the son of central European immigrants, was raised in the slums of New York, and became determined to be a success in North American terms. As Lucy observes, he is "the lonely, undersized foreign boy transferring to the new world the hatred of the old" (287). Bratian is a new version of the self-made man: not an inventor, industrialist, or financier but the founder of a dynamically successful advertising agency. Bratian "had an authentic money-hunger" (242). His pursuit of wealth was aided by a total lack of ideals or inhibiting moral scruples:

> Bratian sometimes laughed silently as he reflected what a joke it was that nobody except himself seemed to know in his bones that life was completely without meaning, that it was merely a fact and should be treated as such, that the only difference between success and failure was whether you satisfied a longing you had acquired in childhood—or you didn't satisfy it. (247)

Plainly, Bratian's materialistic outlook is influenced not only by the values of the consumer society but also by a cynical reading of psychoanalytic ideas.

Bratian's bleak philosophy represents one extreme of MacLennan's spectrum of failure. Bratian has failed so badly as a human being that he is no longer able to recognize his shortcomings. Bruce Fraser, self-effacing and insecure, is at the opposite end of the scale from Bratian. Bruce's refusal to enter the success race is far less flamboyant than Stephen's erratic rise and fall. Nonetheless, Bruce's deep-seated lack of self-assurance is ultimately the most important feature of MacLennan's diagnosis of Canadian society.

Bruce's retreat from life can be illustrated by considering his reaction to the realization that he is on the verge of falling in love with Lucy, who at that point is still happily married to Stephen:

> With a ruthlessness toward himself which was typical, which in fact was a product of his whole life-training, his will-power took control and crushed the color and the wildly trembling excitement into the hinterland of his mind. Lucy was married. Therefore it was impossible to fall in love with her. Therefore he did not love her. Therefore he must think of something else. (210)

Bruce's puritan heritage is the force that dictates this self-denial; his reticent approach to life makes him a typical representative of his country. Stephen tells Lucy that Canadians are "different—as if you'd never got started, somehow. You don't make the money you should because you don't think big enough. You're too content to take what people give you. You're too polite" (107-8). Bruce's self-abasement puzzles Stephen's sister Marcia, who remarks to Lucy: "Strange people you are—both of you. Are you all like that where you come from—shy and self-critical and under the surface as passionate as hell?" (311).

As another of MacLennan's representative Canadians, Lucy does not blame her husband when her marriage begins to turn sour, but instead reproaches herself: "Part of her failure lay simply in her incapacity to keep him amused, in not being able to feel enthusiastic about the kind of success he had made, in not sharing the same values" (301). Lucy doesn't realize that Stephen's real problem is that all his life he has "been haunted by the feeling that he could never measure up to the men his father has tamed and mastered" (71). Stephen has never outgrown the fear of displeasing his powerful, demanding father. A perpetual adolescent, he seeks reassurance of his importance through an affair with Gail Beaumont and tries to escape his problems through alcohol. Stephen's difficulties also have a broader significance. Bratian tells Lucy that Stephen's conduct is simply another example of the "American disease" (284). And Bruce Fraser is sorry to see Lucy involved in "this routine sequel to the modern American love story" (341).

The Cameron and Lassiter families are obviously symbols of the national histories of Canada and the United States. The Cameron house

> was one of the oldest properties in Grenville, built by a Massachusetts judge who had been driven out of New England at the time of the American Revolution, owned by his descendants ever since. It was a Scotsman who had married into the family three generations before who had added the brown paint and the harshness, for the Scotch and the Scotch-Irish who had flooded into Ontario in the wake of the original Loyalist settlers had roughened everything they touched. It would be another hundred years before any part of English-speaking Canada could hope to be rid of what they had done to it. (4–5)

Stephen Lassiter's family incorporates two significant strands of the American tradition. Stephen's mother represents inherited social position and traditional values. She stems from "the Gresham family, old New England stock with ship-owners, mill-masters, clergymen, and finally with intellectuals behind her" (66). His father, on the other hand, was a self-made man and proud of it; he "had been born on a dirt farm forty miles west of St. Louis" (67). Stephen's grandfather had once founded a town on the Kansas plains, which Lucy and Stephen visit on a holiday trip. The town has fallen into decay, but seeing it is an instructive experience for Lucy:

> She learned then a little of what it meant to be an American with a press of lonely, hopeful men behind you, still carrying within yourself something of the belief which had brought Thomas Lassiter from Missouri, and his father to Missouri from Ohio, and behind him the long line of lean men threading west out of New England, no poetry in them, no music, but the necessity of believing that westward things were better, over every mountain a valley richer than the last, carrying wherever they went the qualities that made them unlike any other people who had ever lived, the great refusal to be satisfied, to rest and sit down, the unwillingness to be content which was as hard as a rock in the soul. First the Lord had hounded them, and when the Lord grew remote, they had hounded themselves. (277–78)

In his essays MacLennan habitually personifies Canada as a woman; in *The Precipice* he represents Canada as the sheltered small-town girl Lucy Cameron and represents the United States as the brash, athletic, and boyish Stephen Lassiter. Stephen, the American, jolts Lucy out of her withdrawal from life and offers her an exciting new world of experience. However, he puts her through a conventional humiliation as a neglected and then betrayed wife. Lucy retreats to her Canadian home, but eventually realizes it is her moral duty to return to Stephen and attempt to help him put together his shattered life. The outcome of the novel seems meant to show the redemption of a faltering American dream by an infusion of Canadian morality.

Throughout the novel, the failures of nerve exhibited by the Canadian characters are attributed to the residual influence of Calvinist theology. From adolescence, Lucy "sensed that for the rest of their lives she and Jane would bear the weight of the merciless religion" (52) passed on by their father. The same religious legacy has marked Bruce Fraser, so that he retreats from recognizing his incipient attraction to Lucy. The chief embodiment of the Calvinist ethos in the present generation is Lucy's slightly older sister Jane, who already rules the Cameron household as an overbearing matriarch. In good Calvinist fashion, "it was one of Jane's talents to create at will an atmosphere in which everyone around her felt guilt" (103).

One effect of lingering American putitanism is an attitude that can be described as the Hemingway syndrome. When Marcia converts to Catholicism, she reports that her religious instructor has told her, "The only morality Protestants understand any more is pride in being able to take it" (307). Marcia's phrasing echoes a satiric discussion that Heather Methuen conducts in *Two Solitudes*. Thinking about her favorite works of contemporary fiction, Heather notices that the authors are all men who portray "a man's dream-world" in which "everything was so lousy there was nothing you could do but take it: you could be a socialist and then the police proved their brutality by beating you up; you got some kind of venereal disease but you could take it." The men in these books were all "bitter, close-mouthed and inarticulate, with chips on their shoulders but sexually as potent as Hercules." Women had a particularly rough time in these books. Only the bitches survived; the nice girls got pregnant and died in childbirth or were killed in some other way. These deaths, Heather notices, are presented from the man's perspective rather than the woman's: "And always it was tough for the man, standing by your bed close-mouthed and too manly to say anything while you died, but before the lights faded out you at least knew that he could take it too."[5]

This is the very attitude Stephen displays when he tries to justify his neglect of Lucy:

What was the matter with New York, for Christ's sake? Was it his fault if Lucy hadn't been able to adjust herself to life down here? The United States set the pace for the world. The world could take it or leave it. He had to take it himself, didn't he? Gail had to take it. God damn it, a hundred and forty million Americans took it—and liked it. (316–17)

Stephen's attitude is the end result of a long secularization of the sense of sin. But the secular outlook offers no way out. Even the strictest Calvinist could hope to be saved through God's grace, but the modern man can only stoically endure the cosmic injustice of the universe. Bruce Fraser reflects, doubtless with Hemingway in mind, "The most famous books of the century swam in evil, all of them, right down to puny imitators like himself, swallowing the whole materialistic fallacy which maintained that to dissect evil is the same as to practice good" (332–33).

A particular instance of the "materialistic fallacy" that is examined in *The Precipice* is Freudian psychology. Marcia expounds the objections to the psychoanalytic viewpoint when she explains the reasons for leaving her own analyst:

"Some psychoanalysts still believe in religion, but he doesn't. He told me any religious impulses I had were simply residual desire to return to the security of my mother's womb, and I told him that was the very *last* place I wanted to go. So I asked myself, if a psychoanalyst is as much a materialist as his patient, what's the good of going to him? It's like being sick from a prussic acid and trying to cure yourself by swallowing the whole bottle." (306)

MacLennan deprecates Marcia's psychiatrist because he merely gave her "a strong sense of guilt and a feeling of remorse for having had three husbands without conceiving a single child" (239). And Marcia satirically remarks: "If Jesus Christ appeared today, we'd send him to a psychoanalyst to get rid of his maladjustments" (217).

However, MacLennan's criticism of Freudian thought comes only after several passages that seem to use psychoanalytic ideas to explain the mental condition of the novel's characters. Somewhere in the course of writing *The*

Precipice, MacLennan seems to have changed his mind about psychoanalysis, and he has not fully removed the traces of his previous attitude. A Freudian outlook makes the narrator observe of Abel Lassiter, "It is hardly reasonable to believe that any man will do things necessary to make a million or more dollars unless he has some childhood dream to lead him on" (69). Jane's repressed personality is linked to her thwarted sexuality: "One would expect her to be at her best in a Bach fugue, but it was only in these slow movements of Beethoven, where religion mingled with a deeply sublimated sexuality, that Jane really found herself in music" (119). When Lucy is uncertain about her developing relationship with Stephen. Matt McCunn, one of MacLennan's most vehemently antipuritan spokesmen, urges her, "Why don't you get in bed with the big bastard?" (160). Lucy herself explains that "the real reason why she spent so many hours over her plants was because she had no children" (42). Stephen's character is said to be shaped by his early relationship with his father, and his later womanizing is explained by Marica as a search for a mother substitute: "Stephen's been hunting female approval ever since he left home. He got it there, but only off and on" (310).

As an alternative to Freudian thought, MacLennan eventually proposes a return to traditional religious belief. The clearest instance is Marcia's conversion to Catholicism. The chief mistake of the modern world, as Marcia sees it, is an exclusive reliance on the materialistic viewpoint. Even before her conversion, she tells Bruce Fraser, "We thought science had arrived to take the place of religion, and we believed the only thing needed to make us good was a good economic system" (217). MacLennan makes plain his belief that Calvinism has emphasized one side of religion—man's sense of sin—at the expense of an equally vital aspect—man's sense of God's love. Lucy realizes that her father's view was very incomplete:

> The other side of the Presbyterian faith, the great and noble side enunciated in the response to the first proposition of the Catechism, struck Lucy with a force she had never felt in church before—*Man's chief end is to glorify God and enjoy him forever!* Her father, she thought smiling, might have wanted to believe that, but he had never felt it safe to take a chance on it. (143)

In the novel's final scene, when Lucy has returned to Stephen, she at last recognizes the depth of Stephen's inherited puritanism. She asks, "Stephen dear—how long are you going to let dead men make you ashamed of yourself?" (371). Lucy commits herself to Stephen once again, for she recognizes the core of integrity within his apparently immoral behavior.

The Calvinist Legacy

The forgiveness she extends to Stephen is the earthly echo of the divine forgiveness she remembers is part of the Christian heritage: "Into her mind floated a scene from her childhood in Grenville, her father reading the morning prayers: 'And by grace are ye saved through faith, not of yourselves; it is a gift of God'" (370).

The ending of *The Precipice* is not wholly satisfactory. Initially, the romance between Stephen and Lucy, like the love stories in MacLennan's first two novels, acts as a framework on which to hang a series of political and social observations—in this case a discussion of the differences between American and Canadian values. But MacLennan's love story soon moves in an unexpected direction. The lovers in the two previous novels had eventually freed themselves from society's restrictions and from parental dominance. But Lucy and Stephen are never really freed from the weight of their past histories.

It would appear that MacLennan, at this stage of his career, is uncertain to what extent the individual can escape the burden of the past and the pressures of society. Much as he desires to believe that individuals can control their own lives, he fears that they are governed by external forces and at times by purely random events. But *The Precipice* points the way to a solution. By turning to a religious viewpoint, MacLennan strives to free himself from an impasse like that which once faced his own fictional alter ego, Paul Tallard. After reading the manuscript of Paul's first novel, Heather Methuen reflects, "The trouble lay in the fact that Paul's emotions and mental analysis had not coalesced." She tells Paul: "Your characters are all naturally vital people. But your main theme never gives them a chance. It keeps asserting that they're doomed."[6] Throughout his first three novels, MacLennan creates characters who are trapped or threatened by political, economic, and social conditions. In his later novels, he seeks a way out of this dilemma, a way in which individuals need not be wholly at the mercy of an arbitrary world.

One feature of *The Precipice* is particularly indicative of the direction MacLennan's writing was to take: the peculiar role assigned to Bruce Fraser. Bruce is one of the many partial self-portraits in MacLennan's novels. He is an intellectual, a student of history, a writer, and for a time a teacher in a private school. Later he combines his interests in politics and writing to produce the kind of personal political journalism at which MacLennan himself excels. MacLennan seems to have endowed Bruce with some of his own innermost fears. For a long time Bruce—like MacLennan himself during the thirties—experiences himself as a failure. Ostensibly Bruce fails through no fault of his own; he is simply a victim of the

Depression. But—again like MacLennan himself—Bruce has internalized the Calvinist sense of guilt so thoroughly that he actually seems to retreat from the world. Bruce seems to feel himself inadequate to meet life's daily challenges, and he denies himself romantic fulfillment by repressing his attraction for Lucy and pursuing the flirtatious but basically frigid Nina. Throughout the novel Bruce is repeatedly contrasted with Stephen. This pairing serves an interesting purpose. By creating what is in effect a doubled main character—one half introverted, one half extroverted—MacLennan is able both to affirm and deny his puritan background; he is able to submit and rebel at the same time. The handling of the doubled characters is not wholly successful in *The Precipice*. Bruce is not sufficiently a participant in the novel's action; he is too much the mere observer. Moreover, some character traits and actions seem to be assigned to the wrong person. Wartime heroism and bodily wounds seem more properly to belong to the physically active, unreflective Stephen Lassiter. Conversely, the rejection from military service on trivial medical grounds and the obvious self-pity underlying so much of Stephen's conduct would sit more comfortably on Bruce Fraser. Nonetheless, the use of a doubled main character offers MacLennan a solution to one of his recurrent problems: the weakness of his supposedly active protagonists. The solution is to create a character like Bruce Fraser, through whose eyes the heroic figure can be observed without being brought so close to the reader that his credibility dissolves. Thus, the pairing of Stephen Lassiter and Bruce Fraser is a trial run for the more successful coupling of George Stewart and Jerome Martell in *The Watch That Ends the Night*. But before MacLennan was ready to create George Stewart, who is a projection of his essential self, he had to return once more to a confrontation with the father he still carried within himself.

Each Man's Son

When *The Precipice* received mixed reviews, especially in Canada, MacLennan felt his fledgling career was in jeopardy. He had not gained the large American audience he had hoped to win with this novel, and he seemed in danger of losing his Canadian following. He responded in the same way he had earlier responded to the impasse created when his initial efforts at fiction had not been published. He turned to his childhood experiences for the setting of his next novel, and he again created a swiftly moving, tightly knit plot.

The Calvinist Legacy 65

But it was not his original intention to write about Cape Breton. After finishing *The Precipice,* he worked for six months on a novel "which had no connection with my childhood or the place where I was born." Then one evening at a party, "I found myself telling what are always called in the rest of Nova Scotia 'Cape Breton stories'—anecdotes apocryphal and otherwise that I had almost forgotten I knew." The next morning, "I put away the novel on which I had spent six months and I have never looked at it again."

Cape Breton stories can deal with many subjects, but one of the favorite topics is the legendary Giant MacAskill, once reputed the world's strongest man. Other stories reflect the island's precarious and often violent way of life. "Some of the tales," MacLennan writes, "have to do with wrecks on the jagged coasts, others [tell] of epic combats in Senator's Corner on Saturday night, others of mighty native prize-fighters whose waywardness lost them world's championships, others again of absurd incidents in the countryside now congealed to legend."[7] Tales of this sort provide the inspiration for many of the incidents contained in *Each Man's Son.* As MacLennan commented in a letter to his publisher, John Gray, "In a sense this is a folk-novel and in the truest sense of the word Cape Breton is a folk country with its own lore."[8]

The use of folk materials makes *Each Man's Son* unique among MacLennan's novels. At times he becomes a more uninhibited storyteller than he is anywhere else in his fiction. A spirit of play that is all too rare in his writing animates the tale of Giant MacAskill that Angus the Barraman tells to young Alan MacNeil:

"Nobody that effer lived anywhere wass so strong as Angus MacAskill of St. Ann's, who wass four hundred and twenty-five pounds of bone and muscle, and wass so strong he did not haff to fight to prove it. . . ."

"He showed it once and for all the day the Yankee sea captain put into St. Ann's for water and boasted there wass stronger men in the Boston States than they wass in Cape Breton. . . ."

"When that sea captain laughed, the giant did not think it wass funny at all. So he stood up and he looked across the bay and measured the distance, and the bay wass so wide not even a rainbow could cover it. Then MacAskill put owt his hands, and he picked that sea captain up, and he bent over and he pointed his ass across the bay like a big gun, and nobody effer saw the like again of what happened then. For MacAskill fired such a blow owt of his ass that the sea captain sailed most of the way across the bay, and landed with a big splash right in front of Englishtown. He whould haff gone all the way across moreoffer and busted hisself on the beach, but MacAskill wass such a nice man he did not want to hurt him." (162–63)

More than in any other of his novels, MacLennan integrates the vigorous dialogue of his uneducated characters into the fabric of *Each Man's Son*. The salty vitality hitherto given only to single characters such as Captain Yardley or Matt McCunn is allowed to permeate an entire fictional community; and there is no condescension in MacLennan's presentation of the brawling, hard-drinking miners.

But the creation of an appealing folk novel is not MacLennan's primary purpose in *Each Man's Son*. Rather, he means to continue the analysis of Calvinism he began in *The Precipice*. In the letter to his publisher referred to above, he explained that his "mortal quarrel with Calvinism . . . was that it inculcated into children the idea that God was each man's personal enemy, and that a man committed a sin merely by existing." The novel's examination of Calvinism also has a personal significance. MacLennan acquired his familiarity with Calvinism by growing up under the tutelage of Dr. Sam. In *Each Man's Son,* he conducts a more open scrutiny of his feelings toward his father than he has hitherto allowed himself.

The protagonist of the novel is Dr. Daniel Ainslie, who, like MacLennan's own father, is a colliery doctor in Cape Breton. MacLennan has described how Dr. Sam "used to rush from his surgery, seat himself at a desk, and with a huge lexicon beside him he would grimly translate pages of Latin and Greek classics."[9] In a similar way, Dr. Ainslie uses every moment he can snatch from a busy medical practice to flog himself through a few more lines of Homer, which he laboriously translates from the Greek. This portrait of Dr. Ainslie can be viewed in two ways. On the one hand, MacLennan is creating a character who embodies his attempt to understand his own father. On the other hand, Dr. Ainslie's personality has in its turn been shaped by the teachings of a sternly Calvinist father; therefore, Dr. Ainslie's attitude toward his father is in part a portrait of MacLennan's feelings toward Dr. Sam.

In *The Precipice,* when Lucy Cameron contemplated the Calvinist forebears who had blighted her father's life and whose influence threatened to dominate her own existence, she told herself, "Knowledge was the only power in the world which could undo the chain of evil men left behind them" (53). In *Each Man's Son,* MacLennan shows that knowledge alone will not bring freedom from what he calls in his prologue the "ancient curse" of Calvinism. What is needed is a compassionate understanding of the fears that had led one's ancestors to welcome the forbidding Calvinist outlook. Calvinism is a pessimistic philosophy, a philosophy of desperation, based on the premise that human nature—one's own included—is intrinsically evil and constantly in need of external regulation. Strict

The Calvinist Legacy 67

Calvinism is therefore based on fear of oneself. Only by understanding the weakness as well as the strength of that "old Calvinist," his father, can Dr. Ainslie release himself from bondage to a self-imposed demand for an impossible perfection. And as he narrates Dr. Ainslie's story, MacLennan is exercising the shade of another "old Calvinist," namely the father whose outlook has dominated his life.

There is a dark side to the Cape Breton community MacLennan portrays, for the miners' vitality and delight in life, expressed so forcefully in their vigorous language, are bottled up by the strictness of the theology under which they live. Their brawling is caused by an instinctive energy that can find no constructive outlet. Their drinking is a way of seeking to obliterate their awareness of sin. Their minister wonders whether "it was going too far to warn the congregation against taking the promises of the New Testament too literally. For if God was love, what was to be done about Jehovah?" (41). Even the local saloon keeper wonders if a stomachache could be "sent as a punishment for sin" (41). And the witchlike Mrs. MacCuish, in response to Alan MacNeil's question, "What is sin?" can only exclaim, "What are you your ownself but a lump of it whateffer?" (153).

Calvinism shadows the entire community, but it falls with particular intensity on Dr. Ainslie, making him a driven, unhappy man. He takes on a killing work load, which he increases by his self-imposed task of reading Homer. He is trying to drown out a sense of inadequacy, instilled in him by his father, a ferociously strict Presbyterian. Dr. Ainslie's sense of unworthiness is so ingrained that it persists even after he has decided that God is only a human invention. His friend Dr. Dougald MacKenzie tells him: "You may think you've rejected religion with your mind, but your personality has no more rejected it than dyed cloth rejects its original color. . . . It may sound ridiculous to say, in cold words, that you feel guilty because you're alive, but that's what you were taught to believe until you grew up" (63).

Dr. Ainslie has learned to distrust anything that is easy or pleasurable. One measure of his joyless outlook is provided when he listens to Mollie MacNeil's skillfully told "Cape Breton story" about the eccentricities of a local magistrate, and can only respond curtly, "This town has far too many liars in it" (33). In particular, Dr. Ainslie feels guity over the sexual desire that draws him to his wife Margaret. "There was Margaret—he felt before her, guilty in his soul. Why again? Merely because, when he had married her, he had been so swayed by sexual desire?" (64). He turns away from his wife, precisely because he still loves and desires her. Although he finds her naked body "tantalizingly lovely, it was unbelievably beautiful, yet he had never seemed able to reach its inner warmth or to feel that he had come home to her" (40). Dr. Ainslie knows he is blighting his own life and his wife's life as well, but he is powerless to feel or behave otherwise. It does no good to tell himself that he is "a physician, a learned man of forty-two years, and he no longer believed in hell and damnation" (64). As Dr. MacKenzie tells him, "Dan you haven't forgotten a single word you've ever heard from the pulpit or from your own Presbyterian father" (63).

Dr. Ainslie and his wife have no children. At first, Dr. Ainslie postponed having a family because he feared children would interfere with his career. More recently, he has had to perform a hysterectomy on his wife. However, he is beginning to wish he had a son: "To work as he did now was senseless. To work for a son's future would give purpose to the universe" (85). He soon attaches this wish to a specific boy, Alan MacNeil, the son of the absent boxer Archie MacNeil. He knows his own life is blighted, but he hopes he can teach Alan to avoid his mistakes. Above all, he hopes a son will open new possibilities in a world that, for Dr. Ainslie, is becoming more and more constraining. "A man's son is the boy he himself might have been, the future he can no longer attain. For him, Alan was that boy" (183). Actually, Dr. Ainslie's desire for a son is an expression of his rebellion against the feeling of being trapped in a world where his own life seems to have no significance. He has rejected his father's God, but found no other values to believe in. As a result, his own life is without purpose. He wants a son in order to put meaning back into his own life. As Dr. MacKenzie tells him: "You aren't looking for a son, Dan. You're looking for a God" (189).

Dr. Ainslie's search for a son generates one of MacLennan's most neatly constructed plots. The first half of the book explains Dr. Ainslie's peculiar bondage to the ideas of his father. At the book's mid-point, a "chance" meeting with Alan MacNeil and his mother suggests a solution to Dr. Ainslie: he can make Alan his son. The second half of the novel traces the surprising route by which Dr. Ainslie's dream is realized. Each half of the novel has at its center a scene in which Dr. Ainslie is sagely advised by the kindly Dr. MacKenzie. Each of these scenes is linked with one of the operations that provide some of the book's most striking imagery. In the first half, Dr. MacKenzie discusses the hysterectomy that Dr. Ainslie performed on Margaret; in the second half, the conversation with Dr. MacKenzie is preceded by the appendectomy that Dr. Ainslie performs on Alan MacNeil. Halfway through the novel, Dr. Ainslie, with the aid of the euphoria induced by the idea of gaining Alan as his son, performs a life-giving brain operation. At the novel's end, however, there is not an operation but rather an outburst of murderous violence.

Clearly, this story raises questions about the ethics of Dr. Ainslie's conduct. He wants to commit what amounts to an act of kidnapping. Dr. Ainslie tries to convince himself that his motives are irreproachable: "He told himself that it was a crime for a boy such as Alan to be raised with no future but the mines. Any man with a simple sense of humanity would do what he could to prevent such a boy from being sent into the pits. It was only his plain duty to do what he could" (134). Yet in his more candid moments, he realizes he is "trying to deny Alan's mother, to disregard her, to dismiss her as of no importance" (190). Moreover, the plot of the book seems to question Dr. Ainslie's conduct, for he acquires Alan as his son only at a great expense of human life.

The story makes prominent use of MacLennan's typical device of doubling characters. Dr. Ainslie's ferociously strict father is balanced by the sympathetic Dr. MacKenzie, "the only person in the whole of Cape Breton whom he honored totally and without question" (55). Dr. Ainslie turns to Dr. MacKenzie for advice and reassurance as he never could have turned to his own father. Dr. Ainslie himself is paired with the wandering boxer, Archie MacNeil. Like Dr. Ainslie, Archie is deeply marked by the Calvinist heritage, though he can rebel only physically rather than intellectually. Archie's loneliness expresses "the primitive sadness of his whole race" (108). Dr. Ainslie sees himself as a far more suitable father for Alan than Archie can ever be, but the two men are really opposite sides of the same coin.

MacLennan's narrative technique in *Each Man's Son* is conventional, but skillfully executed. He uses the omniscient narration that is by now habitual with him, but for the great majority of the book he stays within the mind of one or another of his characters. There are few passages where a completely detached observer comments on the action or the characters. Indeed, the book's most conspicuous passage of direct authorial comment is both instrusive and unnecessary. Late in the novel an all-knowing voice intones:

> If God looked down on them that summer, the kind of God their ministers had told them about, He must have been well pleased, for by the summer's end all of them except Alan were conscious of their sins. Longing to do the best, they had discovered there is no best in this world. Yearning for love, they had found loneliness. Eager to help one another, they had made each other wretched. Dreaming of better lives, they had become discontented with the lives they led. (200)

The passage is superfluous: it merely summarizes what has already been conveyed by the action of the novel. And in the next paragraph, the mention of the impending First World War seems a clumsy instance of MacLennan laying on his irony with a trowel.

MacLennan's interjection of a godlike narrator weakens the intensity and immediacy he is trying to achieve in this novel. *Each Man's Son* is a book in which the reader can care about the main characters as he seldom can in MacLennan's previous novels. Too often, the earlier protagonists wore their symbolic roles pinned to their sleeves; their individual personalities were not sufficiently developed. In *Each Man's Son,* MacLennan's broad statement—a condemnation of Calvinism's effects on the sensitive individual—arises effectively from the intensity with which he has portrayed a particular character's situation. Didactic authorial comments are merely a distraction from Dr. Ainslie's personal story.

MacLennan's personal emotions are woven into the novel in a particularly intimate way. In an important sense, *Each Man's Son* is a book about MacLennan's father. At the most obvious level, MacLennan is pointing out his father's shortcomings. His portrayal of Dr. Ainslie is often critical. Ainslie is emotionally cold toward his wife, he is self-centered, and he is oblivious to the needs or the rights of others unless they are his patients. Yet the novel supplies an explanation for Dr. Ainslie's conduct which enables the reader to understand and even to pity him. MacLennan clearly admires Dr. Ainslie's self-discipline, even as he deprecates some of its consequences. Moreover, Dr. Ainslie is a superb physician: "He was one of those rare doctors who invariably seem able to take a patient's ills upon themselves" (27) and magically bolster the patient's will to live.

Indeed, to some readers it may seem that MacLennan has unrealistically idealized Dr. Ainslie's medical skills. This question is discussed in a talk MacLennan delivered shortly after *Each Man's Son* was published. He reports that one friend of his, a doctor, "told me the book had made him so angry he had thrown it across the room. According to him I had committed the usual layman's crime. I had not only idealized the character of the doctor; I had idealized the profession itself."[10] MacLennan expresses surprise at this reaction, for he insists he has not idealized doctors. The significant point here is that MacLennan is clearly wrong and his doctor friend is absolutely correct. MacLennan does idealize doctors in the following account of a difficult brain operation, brilliantly performed by Dr. Ainslie under almost primitive conditions:

> He did perform a great operation. For three and a quarter hours his fingers seemed endowed with the power of thought, while Doucette beside him assisted

flawlessly, administering only a touch of anesthetic at the beginning, stopping it when the instruments entered the cerebral areas where pain does not exist, resuming again at the finish when Ainslie replaced the broken fragments of bone, fitted them together and sealed them. If total concentration on a healing task is a form of holiness, the two doctors were saints during that period. For the first time in his life Ainslie worked successfully below the cortex of the brain. Operating from intuition as much as from exact knowledge, he performed a work of such art that Doucette's eyes glowed with excitement. (125)

It appears certain that the conditions of this operation are loosely based on the conditions of the final operation that Dr. Sam ever performed. MacLennan says in an interivew:

> He [Dr. Sam] was a helluva good surgeon. He was the only person east of Montreal who could do a labyrinth operation, which is practically a brain operation. He'd gone to Vienna and learned how to do it. He died as a result of his last operation when he was dragged on a sleigh in a winter blizzard into the fields somewhere near Windsor, Nova Scotia to operate on a farm table. He came back and had a stroke the next day.[11]

Even in death, Dr. Sam set his son an example of unselfish service that was impossible to match. But in *Each Man's Son,* MacLennan turns Dr. Sam's final operation into the start of a new life for Dr. Ainslie. MacLennan has, by means of his novel, resurrected Dr. Sam and continued an interrupted conversation.

MacLennan's view of doctors can be clarified if we examine the anecdote with which he concludes the talk referred to above. MacLennan's story concerns "an eminent surgeon who was one of the most respected, able and dignified figures in his community." This doctor "insisted on taking a leave of absence every year. Every November he went away for three weeks," on the pretext of attending medical conventions in distant cities. MacLennan explains:

> Because I was a doctor's son, I found out (naturally after the man was dead) what he really did on these trips. This saintly, dignified man always went to Boston. There he registered under an assumed name in a disreputable hotel, ordered a case of whiskey sent up to his room, and when that was consumed, ordered another. Squalid, unkempt and unshaven, he used occasionally to issue forth to the streets and make the round of the bars for conversation. Then he would go back to his room and drink himself unconscious. When his three weeks' vacation was up, he came home, as dignified, aloof and competent as ever, but inwardly purified.[12]

It seems reasonably certain that this unnamed doctor was not MacLennan's father. But the doctor's exact identity hardly matters, for MacLennan is presenting him as a representative medical man. In his talk, MacLennan insists that doctors felt themselves to be a group set apart from other men, and he attributes their sense of isolation to the burden of having to take full responsibility for life-and-death decisions. Doctors must present a facade of perfect competence to the world, while inwardly sensing acutely their own fallibility. The anonymous doctor's annual binge was his way of purging the tensions built up by a year-long masquerade of omniscience.

MacLennan credits his father with a dark side, but he insists that Dr. Sam repressed this aspect of his nature, avoiding liquor because he was "afraid of himself."[13] By creating Dr. Ainslie, whose self-control is as ferocious as Dr. Sam's, MacLennan is suggesting to himself that his father had found no satisfactory way of venting the pressures of his profession, and no outlet for the less exalted side of his nature. The parable about the unnamed doctor's yearly bender is meant as a warning that everyone needs to allow his baser self an outlet. MacLennan's father failed to do this and became the stern, unyielding figure MacLennan knew. Such, at any rate, is the diagnosis MacLennan projects into the action of *Each Man's Son*.

In creating Dr. Ainslie, MacLennan is using his own role as the son of a stern Presbyterian parent to imagine the probable experiences of his father. MacLennan reminds himself that Dr. Sam was himself the product of a Calvinist environment. Thus, he makes Dr. Ainslie, who appears so masterful on the surface, the product of a masterful father, who disguised stubborn and self-serving pride as thrifty self-reliance, who was indirectly responsible for the death of his wife, and who taught Dr. Ainslie to despise women as weak and emotional creatures. As a result of imagining his father's life from within, MacLennan is able to forgive Dr. Sam for his harshness and lack of overt warmth. Indeed, the conclusion of *Each Man's Son* goes further. MacLennan also puts himself into the book in the person of young Alan MacNeil, the boy Dr. Ainslie wishes to adopt. If the novel's conclusion is read from Alan's perspective, it reflects MacLennan's grateful recognition that, despite a forbidding outward manner, his father did want and love him.

This private emotional resolution is given powerful expression in *Each Man's Son*. But there is nonetheless a quality of strain in the book's outcome, for MacLennan has not dealt adequately with another set of ambivalent feelings evoked by the novel's action. Specifically, in MacLennan's fourth novel the uneasiness toward women that is present as a subordinate motif in all his previous novels becomes a conspicuous element in the plot. In particular, *Each Man's Son* explores the uneasy relationship between Dr. Ainslie and his wife Margaret. Dr. Ainslie's view of women is an integral part of the Calvinism that has shaped his outlook. A definite hostility to women is one of the less attractive aspects of Christianity's legacy to Western society. The story of the expulsion from the Garden of Eden has frequently served to rationalize the subordinate role of women in Western culture. Eve yielded to temptation first, then tempted Adam, who explains to God, "The woman who thou gavest to be with me, she gave me of the tree, and I did eat" (Gen 3:12). The story of the Fall has therefore been used to justify a view of women as weaker than men and less capable of rational thought. Moreover, in much Christian thought, women have been considered the source of a carnal desire that is sinful except within narrowly defined boundaries and the satisfaction of which is never to be enjoyed for its own sake. Dr. Ainslie has acquired these attitudes, which were part of his father's Calvinism.

Margaret Ainslie herself, however, embodies a different conception of woman. When she is introduced to the reader, she is cutting flowers in her garden. This scene does not identify her as an Eve-like temptress, but as part of nature. Margaret's outlook has been shaped by a family background very unlike Dr. Ainslie's. Margaret's mother, not her father, dominated her upbringing, and Margaret "had grown up comfortably without worry or struggle. . . . Her mother had reared her with the notion that there was a smooth-edged solution for everything" (171). Margaret is unashamed of her sexuality: "She loved having Dan enjoy her; it was her secret belief that she was very good at making love and she wished Dan would give himself more time to enjoy her properly" (77).

Margaret is not criticized for her easygoing attitude. It is her husband's fear of normal human emotions and physical responses that the novel holds up for critical scrutiny. Dr. Ainslie's innermost wish is often to escape from his present plight by returning to the security he felt during his boyhood in the Margaree Valley before his mother died. Indeed, he feels an attraction to Mollie MacNeil because she reminds him of his mother. "He thought of the expression in Mollie's eyes as she comforted Alan, lost sight of it in a welter of images, then recovered it again. Then it was not Mollie's eyes he was looking into; they were the eyes of his own mother. Mollie and his mother became confused and he was confused with Alan" (189). Dr. Ainslie does not feel sexual desire for Mollie so much as a desire for the undemanding affection his mother once gave him.

Dr. Ainslie carries MacLennan's study of sexuality a stage further than his previous novels do. Several of MacLennan's earlier characters compromised between sexual desire and a desire to remain within the security of the family by falling in love with someone to whom they had close childhood ties. Neil Macrae and Penny Wain were cousins, and were raised in the same house, like brother and sister. In *Two Solitudes,* Paul Tallard and Heather Methuen play together as children when Heather visits her grandfather's farm. In *The Precipice,* Bruce Fraser, who has known Lucy Cameron from childhood, is presented as the man who should have perceived the femininity dormant in Lucy and so forestalled her troubled marriage to Stephen Lassiter. No such compromise is allowed to Dr. Ainslie. He marries a siren and is then ashamed to admit he has been tempted and has fallen. In effect, Dr. Ainslie does not want to take responsibility for his own sexuality; he resists growing up, because he finds adulthood, as defined for him by his father, to be a painfully self-punitive condition. He wishes for a mother rather than a wife, because his wife's sexuality forces him to experience an aspect of his own nature of which he is ashamed.

Dr. Ainslie's sexual guilt exacerbates his guilt over the way he has denied children to Margaret. The operation he performed rendered her sterile. Although Margaret is firmly reassured by Dr. MacKenzie that the operation was a medical necessity, she is actually quite right to question her husband's motives. Symbolically Dr. Ainslie has deliberately denied Margaret the fulfillment she so much desires; he had in effect made destructive love to her with his scalpel. Dr. Ainslie's uneasiness is intensified by his fear of his own feelings. Sex threatens loss of self-control, a destruction of the hard-won image of self-sufficiency he has created for himself in an attempt to satisfy his father's exacting standards. Dr. Ainslie as a child absorbed his father's derogatory attitude toward women. Speaking to Dr. MacKenzie of his mother, Dr. Ainslie says: "My father was always afraid I'd be like her. He warned me often enough, heaven knows. I'm afraid she was a weak character" (187–88). Dr. Ainslie resents his sexual need for Margaret, and even more fundamentally, he resents what that sexual need symbolizes: his own need to love and be loved, his need for other people—in short, the emotional or "feminine" aspects of his own nature.

Dr. Ainslie's emotional side does not stay repressed forever. When it appears, it takes the form of a sudden fondness for the son of the absent Archie MacNeil. Dr. Ainslie's longing for young Alan reaches a crisis when he performs an appendectomy on the boy. Despite its medical

The Calvinist Legacy 75

simplicity, the operation induces a surprisingly great mental stress in the doctor:

> When he was in the hall the strange feeling of being about to perform his first operation settled upon him again. He looked at his hands and saw they were trembling. He stood still and breathed deeply several times, leaned his head back and closed his eyes. Slowly he brought his nerves under control, but when he looked at his hands they were still tighter than they ought to be. (180)

Dr. Ainslie's extreme reaction to such a simple operation can be accounted for only by considering his emotional situation. He has inflicted sterility on his wife by performing an operation; now by saving Alan through another operation, he can symbolically reverse his previous action. The operation is, for Dr. Ainslie, a birth scene: he is claiming Alan as his son.

After the operation, Dr. Ainslie flees to the seaside, where he finds himself "muttering 'No!' over and over again, without knowing what he was saying no against. He was still shaking as if with a malaria chill, then he stopped muttering and shouted 'NO!' as loudly as he could at the empty, noisy space, and suddenly he felt tears burst down his face" (182). Dr. Ainslie is hurling defiance at the empty universe which his loss of faith has left him facing. He defies the ghost of the punitive God in whom he no longer believes, and at the same time he expresses his horror at his growing realization that his life has been a failure. Soon his inner need for meaning overcomes his knowledge that it is wrong to covet another man's son. "He might as well stop trying to bolster his fierce inner pride. He let his mind go where it would, freed of the restraints he had put upon it for so long. He saw Alan growing up, year by year moving to manhood in dignity, himself being a companion to him, helping him, teaching him to be the kind of man he himself was not" (183).

MacLennan would have us believe that his novel ends happily, and that before he acquires Alan as his son, Dr. Ainslie learns wisdom. Before this happens, Dr. Ainslie is faced down by Mollie in a direct encounter, "because he was ashamed of something and she was not" (218). He immediately descends into the blackest despair of his life; however, he emerges emotionally renewed, having "made the discovery that he was ready to go on with life" (220). Supposedly, Dr. Ainslie has found a firm center within himself. Like Yardley, he has faced "ultimate solitude" and refused to believe that the universe is devoid of meaning or pattern. Dr. Ainslie then instructs Margaret to book their passage to Europe, presumably so he can undertake the advanced study he has long contemplated.

But Dr. Ainslie's recovery is not believable. The novel's events seem to suggest that something quite different has happened. The plot of the novel acts out with brutal explicitness Dr. Ainslie's desire to take Alan away from Mollie. At the novel's climax, Louis Camire and Mollie are murdered by Archie, and then Archie dies—all so that Dr. Ainslie may inherit the orphaned Alan. Mollie and Louis Camire both opposed the doctor; now they are dead. The perpetrator of this carnage, Archie MacNeil, is the barely disguised alter ego of the doctor. Both Archie and Dr. Ainslie have rebelled against their constricting backgrounds. Archie channels into his fighting the same violent rebellion against authority that Dr. Ainslie's strict self-control only barely holds in check.

The return of Archie as the incarnation of Dr. Ainslie's murderous impulses is actually foreshadowed in a scene to which Warren Tallman draws attention in his provocative essay "Wolf in the Snow." When Dr. Ainslie flees to the dock after he has operated on Alan, he trips over the drunken miner Red Willie MacIsaac, a notorious brawler. Red Willie is one of those exiled Highlanders who, as Tallman says, are "doomed to wear their vitality away in the dreary Cape Breton mines, [and] rebel like the profound children they are by recourse to the only political action of which they are capable, their endless evening brawls." This same violence is present in Dr. Ainslie, whose veneer of self-control serves "to hold these impulses in check." Of the moment when Dr. Ainslie trips over Red Willie, who then rises over the fallen doctor like a summoned genie, Tallman writes: "When the rhythms of Ainslie's mind and body become separated and he trips and becomes mingled with Red Willie there is reason to believe that 'this living thing . . . beside him' is simply the self behind the mask, the vital, violent being held in check by the civilized surface."[14]

As Tallman astutely points out, Red Willie is at this moment drunkenly mourning Archie's defeat in a boxing match, and in his first words to Dr. Ainslie, he speaks as though with Archie's voice: "There wass dirty tricks in the States last Friday night, and by Cheesus, I am going to kick them back up your ass" (184). Through Red Willie's words, Archie vows vengeance against Ainslie, his rival as Alan's father. But when the confrontation takes place, Dr. Ainslie is the victor:

The crowd saw Ainslie step forward, his bag in his left hand, and then Archie loomed under the overhead light. The doctor and the fighter stopped as they recognized each other. . . .

The Calvinist Legacy 77

At that moment Archie seemed of more than human size. Standing in the doorway with the light over his head, he was a good foot higher than the doctor. In the imaginations of the crowd he was higher still because of what they knew he had done. They saw him draw back his right fist, but only Ainslie was close enough to see and understand the expression in Archie's eyes. They were as full of pleading as the eyes of an overwhipped child. (235-36)

When Dr. Ainslie speaks, Archie's resolution breaks; he falls forward and is caught by Dr. Ainslie.

At the end of *Each Man's Son,* Dr. Ainslie has acquired a son without implicating himself sexually with his wife. Thus, *Each Man's Son* ends ambiguously. The explicit message and the implicit meaning of the action seem to be at odds. Dr. Ainslie is told by Dr. MacKenzie: "You would do well to honor your father less and your mother more. She was a very loving woman" (189). Ostensibly, Dr. Ainslie learns this lesson. However, the plot of the novel acts out a violent antagonism toward women. Nor is Dr. Ainslie's supposed love for Alan at the end of the novel entirely convincing. The doctor seems to adopt Alan in order to create an extension of his own personality, not to further Alan's welfare in a truly loving manner. The sterile Margaret, the murdered Mollie, and Dr. Ainslie's own self-starved mother mutely contradict the notion that he has attained emotional maturity.

The veritable orgy of violence with which *Each Man's Son* ends appears to have been purgative for MacLennan himself. By writing about his own hostility to Dr. Sam, MacLennan cleared the ground for his next novel. *The Watch That Ends the Night* expresses a quietism that has always been part of MacLennan's outlook, but it seems likely that the poise and compassion with which George Stewart confronts a world of confusion and suffering could be reached only by way of a confrontation with the darker emotions such as MacLennan conducts in *Each Man's Son.* Moreover, MacLennan has to deal with his father's turbulent emotional legacy before he can grapple with the increasing stress intruded into his own life by the worsening health of his own wife. In *Each Man's Son,* MacLennan begins to accomplish for himself the task he attributes to Dr. Ainslie in the prologue to his novel. MacLennan confronts "the daemon which has made him what he is" and thereby prepares for his next novel, in which he will express "the other daemon which gives him hope of becoming more than any man can ever be" (ix).

Chapter Five
Requiem and Renewal

MacLennan's working title for his fifth novel was "Requiem." He saw the book as an elegy for a generation whose lives had been shadowed by the Depression, by the Hitler war, and then by the atom bomb and the cold war. In addition, the book was meant as a tribute to MacLennan's wife, for Catherine's fate is modeled on the long ordeal of Dorothy Duncan, which ended when she died at Easter of 1957. MacLennan has said that during the last years of her life, Dorothy Duncan was "like a city under siege, and the end of the siege was as sure as the last shot in a war. She knew it; I knew it; her friends knew it. For the last ten years she lived knowing that on any hour of any day she might die." Despite her physical weakness and several nearly fatal illnesses, MacLennan's wife did not give way to anger or despair. MacLennan says, "During all that time of pain and weakness, with death an imminent certainty, she loved people and life and the world."

Dorothy Duncan's illnesses cut short her promising career as a writer. Instead, she took up painting, which placed less strain on her weakened constitution. In fact, during her final months, she at last found her personal style as an artist. MacLennan says:

> Her pictures were full of joy in a time when the most famous writers of her own country, and the most praised writers of Europe, were devoting their immense technical abilities to the dissection of cowards, drunkards, weaklings, criminals, psychotics, imbeciles, and people whose sole common denominator seems to be a hatred of life and a terror of living.[1]

MacLennan's novel is not as exuberant as Dorothy Duncan's art; but like his wife, MacLennan has used his art to affirm his faith that human life is part of a larger, meaningful pattern. George Stewart speaks for MacLennan when he says, "Remembering the years when she had wrung life and joy out of pain and perpetual exhaustion, I knew, deep inside, that this struggle was not valueless."[2]

Although MacLennan modeled the medical history of his heroine on his own wife's illnesses, his novel is not simply a transposition of his private life into fiction. In many articles on both modern society and modern literature, MacLennan has put forward a strongly antimodernist intellectual and artistic credo. *The Watch That Ends the Night* is the book that most completely and most feelingly translates this personal philosophy into fiction. This is not to label MacLennan's novel a "thesis" book, written as a mechanical illustration of an artistic program. Rather, *The Watch That Ends the Night* is the book in which MacLennan is most fully and most confidently himself. The book's harmonious blending of the emotional and intellectual sides of MacLennan's nature makes it the pinnacle of his achievement.

The Dynamics of Goodness

The success of *The Watch That Ends the Night* owes a great deal to the development MacLennan's style underwent during the 1950s. Throughout the forties, he viewed his occasional articles either as a way of making money or "as a quicker way of telling the world than a novel could do." But in the fifties, he undertook a new kind of journalistic writing when he agreed to contribute regularly to both the *Montrealer* and *Saturday Night*. Writing a regular column demanded a lighter, more personal approach than MacLennan had taken in most of his previous articles. Nonetheless, he reports, "I tried out my temperament on the short essay and found it fitted my needs and pleasures very well."[3] The resulting essays, the best of which are reprinted in *Thirty and Three* and *Scotchman's Return and Other Essays*, are important in their own right, for they represent the high point of MacLennan's career as a writer of nonfiction. But these essays also have a crucial place in the development of MacLennan's career as a novelist, for it was in the pages of the *Montrealer* and *Saturday Night* that MacLennan learned to create the graceful and intimate prose that he brilliantly uses to characterize George Stewart.

From writing these essays, MacLennan learned that a "decent intimacy" between a writer and his audience is an integral part of good writing. Both author and reader must share "the illusion that he is lounging in his library late in the evening of a well-spent day, a glass of beer at his elbow and a personal friend in the opposite chair."[4] MacLennan's awareness of the importance of the writer's control of tone and style was also sharpened by his teaching at McGill, where he gave courses on the modern novel and on the history of English prose. As a result, he began to consider style as well as thematic content when he wrote his critical discussions of modern literature. MacLennan's most thorough examination of the dominant modern style, that fostered by the example of Ernest Hemingway, can be found in his essay "Homage to Hemingway."[5] He draws an analogy between the overhauling of English prose style during the Restoration and Hemingway's stylistic revolution early in the present century. Hemingway "sought by trial and error for a means of setting down with truth and vividness what his five senses told him, knowing that what they told him was much subtler than anything his predecessors had been able to communicate. And he found it." However, Hemingway has applied his purified style to a purpose of which MacLennan cannot entirely approve:

What Hemingway has done has been to restore order and clarity to our use of the English language. But unlike the followers of Dryden, who insisted on clarity as a means to accurate thinking, he has used this classic criterion of style to represent accurate feeling. The style of the eighteenth century produced intellectualism: the style of Hemingway has made sensualism an end in itself.

MacLennan's objection to the Hemingway style is a moral one. The Hemingway style is exquisitely crafted, but socially irresponsible.

MacLennan admits that Hemingway's prose has the "ability to move us and expand our perceptions." Yet the style also has severe limitations. Hemingway "dare not use characters who are thoughtful men, for if he did they would ruin the bare perfection of his style by speaking in a dialogue full of abstract words and by abstaining from doing many of the things a Hemingway character must do in order to give the Hemingway style its full magical effect." Therefore, MacLennan argues, Hemingway cannot create self-consciously reflective and introspective characters, and he cannot cast an intellectual as a major protagonist:

Rational men discuss their own neuroses, they are interested in science, they become involved in a multitude of activities for which the Hemingway style lacks an adequate vocabulary. . . . In short, their minds, their ambitions, their awareness of themselves as coherent, complex personalities involved in a mundane existence make them entirely unsuitable as catalysts for Hemingway.

MacLennan adds, clearly intending to identify a serious omission in Hemingway's outlook, "Such men are even apt to wonder at times how they can save their souls," just as George Stewart wonders how he can save his soul.

MacLennan has consistently expressed strong reservations about the dominant tendency of modern fiction. For example, in an article titled "Changing Values in Fiction," he acknowledges that writers such as Dos Passos, Hemingway, and Mailer have written work of considerable merit.[6] But he feels their books have brought fiction to a spiritual dead end. He dislikes the "total, almost nihilistic pessimism" of Hemingway, and he decries the bleak naturalism of Dos Passos's *U.S.A.* trilogy:

Nowhere in literature, not even in Zola, have human characters been so relentlessly displayed as the mere product of their economic and social environment as in this book. Nowhere, not even in the work of Maxim Gorky has a novel presented a social picture as ugly and bleak and senseless as Dos Passos's portrait of America.

Of Mailer's *The Naked and the Dead* MacLennan writes: "Its will to death is almost absolute. The death-wish which has haunted both our civilization and our literature has never been more eloquently celebrated by any novelist who wrote in the English language." MacLennan's overall complaint, then, is that the modern novel wallows in evil and despair, and offers no hope of an alternative vision.

But MacLennan goes on to argue that "the signs of a really significant change of attitude" have begun to appear in some recent fiction. To support his contention, he cites works by Evelyn Waugh, Graham Greene, and Joyce Cary. But the book on which he pins his greatest hopes is Alan Paton's *Cry, the Beloved Country:*

Alan Paton knows just as much about evil as Mailer does; indeed, he knows a great deal more about it, just as he better understands the true origins of fear, hatred and the destruction of the personality. Yet *Cry, the Beloved County,* tragedy though it is, is a work of tremendous affirmation. For in the character of the old negro preacher, Mr. Kumalo, Paton has done what no writer of our century has yet succeeded in doing within a realistic novel. He has shown an utterly good, Christian, intelligent man involved in a horrible situation, accepting it and rising above it. He has done the hardest thing any writer can ever do: he has shown, in action, the dynamics of goodness itself.

The Watch That Ends the Night can be viewed as MacLennan's own attempt to show "the dynamics of goodness" in operation.

The Watch That Ends the Night

The Watch That Ends the Night is MacLennan's first novel to be written in the first person since the unpublished "A Man Should Rejoice." By using this viewpoint, MacLennan incorporates all the mannerisms and didactic tendencies of his usual omniscient narration into the persona of George Stewart and harnesses them as integral parts of George's personality. MacLennan's use of the first person coincides with periods in his life when the insecurity of the human condition becomes one of his major preoccupations. Omniscient narration usually implies that the world is knowable— if not to the characters then at least to the author. But MacLennan has often doubted whether the individual can understand, let alone control, the world around him. In the later 1930s, when he wrote "A Man Should Rejoice," he could not seem to get his own career under way. In the 1950s, while he was composing *The Watch That Ends the Night,* the recurring illnesses of his wife emphasized his own inability to make the world do his bidding. And later on during the 1970s, when he was writing *Voices in Time,* his reconsideration of twentieth-century history showed him how helpless the individual was to alter the course of a disintegrating Western society.

At the center of MacLennan's most remarkable novel is the very unremarkable personality of George Stewart. The keynote of George's character is insecurity. He tells the reader: "I have never felt safe. Who of my age could, unless he was stupid?" (3). And he adds, "I have never seemed mature to myself" (4). George's deepest longing is for security. He calls himself "bourgeois at heart. What else is a bourgeois but a man who wants a home, some respect from his fellows and a feeling that he has a future and belongs to a human group?" (157). Some readers find George offensively self-pitying; certainly, he repeatedly calls attention to his own slowness in maturing, and he compulsively harps upon his early failures in life. But it is not fair to dismiss George as simply a crybaby.

MacLennan wants readers to experience George's confessions as evidence of sincerity and candor. George's admissions of immaturity and failure are meant to evoke sympathy and, ultimately, identification. MacLennan feels that most people share George's basic insecurity. At the very least, he expects that George will strike a responsive chord in members of his own generation, "whose oldest members passed the barrier of childhood amnesia during the First World War and whose youngest joined the ranks immediately after the Hitler War."[7] George's account of the intellectual and spiritual plight of this generation is really a summary of MacLennan's view of the dilemma of twentieth-century man. In their enthusiasm to be progressive and "modern," George's generation abandoned traditional religious beliefs and tried to find fulfillment exclusively in this world. They made their families their reason for living or "tried to make gods out of political systems, and worship and serve them" (342). George continues:

> But the trouble is that none of these substitutes abides. The time comes when the wife dies, and then what is there? The time comes when children go away. The time comes when the state is seen for what it is—an organization of job-holders.
> Then, though we may deny it, comes the Great Fear. For if a man cannot believe that he serves more than himself, if he cannot believe there is meaning in the human struggle, what are his chances of emotional survival? We may assert that as flies to wanton boys, so are we to the gods who kill us for their sport. But we can't live long believing this. Human dignity forbids it. (342)

This passage describes George's condition as the novel opens. Catherine's illness brings him face to face with "the Great Fear." He discovers that none of his new beliefs are an adequate substitute for the religious certainty he thought he no longer needed.

The subject of *The Watch That Ends the Night* is life lived under a series of debilitating external threats. George is surrounded by people whose habitual response to the external world is evasion. The Montreal establishment take refuge in their sense of tradition and in a blinkered self-righteousness. George's father engages in a series of boyish hobbies and deceives himself that he is working on socially useful inventions. The frustrated young people of the Depression seek in communism a replacement for the certainties—both social and religious—that they have lost; or they try to lose themselves in promiscuous sex. Dr. Bigbee ignores his Canadian surroundings and tries to re-create an English public school. At first, George is simply one more exponent of this outlook. He too takes refuge in evasion when he buries himself in Waterloo School and wallows in self-pity. Later, he uses his devotion to Catherine as an escape from the world.

However, MacLennan's fundamental message in *The Watch That Ends the Night* is that there is no real escape from ultimate issues. No matter where or how you hide, the world will find you out. The most pressing and disturbing issue of all, MacLennan's novel suggests, is mortality. The three main characters must all confront their own mortality or that of someone close to them. All three learn that, faced with death, we are all equal—each individual becomes Everyman. As Jerome tells George: "Each one of us is everybody, really. What scares us is just that. We want so much to be ourselves, but the time comes when we find we're everybody, and everybody is afraid" (366).

The main action of *The Watch That Ends the Night* is the completion of George Stewart's slow and belated growth to maturity. At the time the novel opens, George thinks he has attained serenity. He tells us, "That evening I was happy" (3). He even feels he has overcome his congenital insecurity: "That winter I truly thought I had begun to relax for the first time since I was a boy. I thought I had come to terms with myself and with the peculiar fate which controlled me owing to my wife. I even thought I might have become self-confident" (4). But his contentment is really an illusion, for he has not fully accepted the fate that hangs over his wife:

> I had made Catherine the rock of my life. As a boy, at least for a time, I had been religious and believed that God cared for me personally. In the Thirties I had said to myself: There is no God. Now I had Catherine and Catherine's fate and that winter, feeling confident of being equal to it, I said to myself: "What difference does it make if there is no God? Or, if God exists, why worry if He is indifferent to justice?"
>
> For on account of Catherine I could not believe that if there is a God He is just. (6)

George has tried to find refuge in Catherine. But such a course of action places humanity in opposition to the rest of the cosmos. No human being, however loving, can dominate the universe. Therefore, George's happiness is built on an insecure foundation, which is further weakened by the uncertain state of Catherine's health. When Jerome returns, it becomes his mission to teach George a more profound view of life—a view incorporating death as part of life, rather than seeing it as the final enemy.

In *The Watch That Ends the Night*, MacLennan at last does justice to the love story he tried to tell in each of his first three published novels. In *Barometer Rising* and *Two Solitudes*, the romance took second place to the social background against which events were being played out. In *The Precipice*, MacLennan flanked Lucy Cameron with the passive Bruce Fraser and the active Stephen Lassiter. However, he forced Lucy to make a choice between her admirers. In effect, Lucy had to content herself with a one-sided figure, a partial personality. No such choice is imposed in *The Watch That Ends the Night*. The plot makes Catherine the wife first of

Jerome, then of George. To each man, Catherine is an idealized image of woman, a Jungian anima figure, seen as the personification of all that is benign, reassuring, and loving in the world.

As the story unfolds, Catherine changes her nature. To the impetuous Jerome, she is sensuous and passionate; to George, she is a martyrlike figure, virtually a saint. Her debilitating illness spiritualizes her sufficiently to allow for her possession by the sensitive and fearful George. George and Jerome can be seen as two aspects of a single personality, so that the novel becomes, as Elspeth Cameron says, "a modern psychomachia, or drama of the soul."[8] Jerome is the heroic figure George would have liked to be. George participates only vicariously in Jerome's adventures; therefore, he is able to deny any complicity in Jerome's emotional outbursts and sexual escapades. When George marries Catherine, he can tell himself that he is simply picking up the pieces left in disarray by Jerome's irresponsible conduct. But George would have behaved as Jerome did, if George had possessed the self-confidence to do so.

George undertakes what is really a form of the traditional heroic quest. His story is ultimately a tale of descent and return, an enactment of the archetypal pattern of death and rebirth. Jerome's arrival triggers George's descent into a troubled sea of memories; the story of Jerome's childhood, prominently located at the center of the novel, brings George face to face with the most basic and brutal facets of human nature. Having broadened his own awareness by vicariously sharing Jerome's experiences, and having had his self-confidence bolstered by Catherine's loving approval, George is ready for the next stage of his journey, an encounter with the negative side of his own personality.

The novel enacts a complex series of variations on MacLennan's favorite family-centered plot. The story explores a number of ways in which families can go wrong; then it asserts that healing is nonetheless possible for the children of those families. George starts with weak parents, but acquires strong surrogate parental figures. Jerome, on the other hand, starts with a domineering mother and acquires a set of obligingly compliant foster-parents. Throughout much of the novel, George and Jerome also experience society as a sort of collective parent. At first they accept society's viewpoint as correct; later they rebel against the prevailing orthodoxy; but eventually they learn to think for themselves and draw their ideas and indeed their conception of themselves from within, without regard to society.

George's natural parents are weak almost to the point of nonexistence. The strongest adult figure in George's early life is his imperious Aunt

Agnes, who bullies his parents and endows George with a sense of his own inadequacy:

> "George," said Aunt Agnes after a time, "I suppose you are aware that the time has come for you to think seriously about your future?"
> "I have been thinking about it."
> "Indeed? What do you intend to be?"
> "I don't know yet, Aunt Agnes."
> "What do you think you could be successful at?"
> "Well I guess there'll be quite a few things."
> "There will *not* be quite a few things, George. You would be useless in business. Business does not attract you, does it?"
> "No."
> "Well? I can't see you as a lawyer. You lack the kind of intelligence and drive for the law, and you would quickly be bored by it. There is only one profession where I can imagine you even earning a living, and that's schoolmastering. In the *right* kind of school, of course." (72)

George is vulnerable to this kind of intimidation because his father has not provided a strong masculine role model, but has remained a child in thought and deed. Indeed, George says his parents "turned into a pair of frightened children at the arrival of an aunt" (70). Later on, when the only job George can secure is as schoolmaster at the second-rate Waterloo School, his sense of failure is confirmed.

George becomes involved in an unusual triangular relationship with Catherine and her husband Jerome Martell. Although George and Catherine are virtually the same age, George looks upon Catherine as though she were older and more experienced than himself, and he tells us, "in a motherly way she professed to feel responsible for my future" (157). He also remarks, "I had come to think of Jerome as a protector, almost as a substitute for the father I never had except in the biological sense" (151). It is no wonder George accepts Jerome as a substitute father and Catherine as a substitute mother: those places in his life were never properly filled by his own parents. While George is becalmed at Waterloo School, Catherine and Jerome help him to find his way to a new life. "Catherine and Jerome took me in," he reports, "and they restored my soul. They let me become a kind of uncle to Sally, then in her sixth year; they introduced me to their friends and to their friends' interests and slowly I began to believe I might be more than an usher in that school of Dr. Bigbee's" (149). Jerome starts George's new life by recommending him for a job with the CBC. As a result, George says, "For the first time in my life I had a real job. For the first time in my life I became more than a cipher" (293).

George's eventual marriage to Catherine is the fulfillment of an oedipal dream of union with a maternal female. Yet in a sense George still guards himself from the responsibility of assuming full manhood. He chooses a wife whose physical condition limits her sexuality and thereby shields himself from taking on a full masculine role. Moreover, his attitude to Catherine is strangely exalted. He occasionally affirms the existence of his sexual desire, but we are not quite sure we should believe him. George is not Jerome, who could say yes to life at whatever risk to Catherine's weakened heart. George sees Catherine not as a wife but as a divine mother.

If, in George Stewart, MacLennan has projected most of his deepest fears and anxieties, in Jerome Martell he projects his heroic fantasies. Jerome is an amalgam of all the strong, apparently confident figures MacLennan has known or heard about. He is a surgeon, like MacLennan's father; he has a social conscience and acts upon it, like Dr. Norman Bethune; and he has the intangible healing quality that MacLennan found in his own Montreal physician, Dr. Reuben Rabinovitch.[9] The story of Jerome Martell is neatly handled in the novel as a sort of counterpoint to George's more mundane life history. At a personal level, Jerome's story enacts in overt form the strong emotions that are repressed in a life such as George leads. At a symbolic level, Jerome's story serves as a link with Canada's historic past, for Jerome enters civilization by fleeing down river in the canoe that was the voyageurs' means of transportation. His story therefore contributes an almost allegorical dimension to MacLennan's novel, for he becomes a modern reincarnation of the central figure in what has been seen as the fundamental "Canadian myth," that of the voyageur.[10]

Above all else, however, Jerome's story is one of MacLennan's most striking presentations of the explosively strong emotions that can exist within the family. Like Dr. Ainslie's story, Jerome's story examines the consequences of a childhood dominated by an oppressive and unloving parent, who despises the opposite sex. Jerome reports that his mother "hated men as a group and despised them, too. 'They're no good,' she used to say to me I don't know how many times. 'All they want is one thing. That and drink is all they want. And they're all the same'" (176). Nevertheless, it happened that "cyclically, this man-hating female required a man, and when she wanted one she took him" (176). The sex life of Jerome's mother rings another variation of MacLennan's recurrent oedipal triangle, for Jerome habitually sleeps in the same bed as his mother, except for the occasional nights when she invites a strange man into her bed.

The guest of Jerome's mother on the night of her murder is the Engineer, a man whose sullen and unfriendly exterior conceals a longing for human companionship:

> The Engineer he had feared so much began talking in a low, earnest stream of conversation, talking about himself, and how lonely he was and how wretched was his life, and how different everything would be if she would go away with him. Jerome could only partly hear his words, and hardly any of them could he remember, but he knew that of all the lonely men in the camp this was the loneliest of all, and he yearned for some gentleness to come into his mother's voice in place of the withholding silence or the sneer he was afraid would come if the Engineer continued to talk like this. He wanted the Engineer to break through his mother's refusal to some kindness inside, to some safe kindness inside. (180)

In other words, at this moment the Engineer's feelings are very much a projection of Jerome's own loneliness and longing for affection from his mother. Thus, when his mother mocks the Engineer, Jerome attacks her in spirit just as surely as the Engineer attacks her physically:

> The man began to curse the woman in a stream of obscenity using every word Jerome had ever heard the men apply to the women they called whores. There was a short struggle, the pant of his mother's breath, then a loud smack as she hit him across the face and Jerome thought: Please, please don't let her do that again! (181)

Jerome's flight from the Engineer and his escape down the river are therefore as much a flight from himself—a flight from his own sense of guilt—as a flight from any actual physical danger. The episode has acted out in terrifyingly literal form a child's worst imaginings about the nature of the sexual act. As a result of this dramatic initiation into knowledge of sexuality, Jerome has prematurely but irrevocably embarked on the river of life.

The couple who adopt Jerome are the very antithesis of those who have hitherto dominated his life:

> He was a thin little man with the kindliest, funniest face Jerome had ever seen, with crowsfeet smiling out from the corners of his blue eyes and a gray goat's tuft on a pointed chin. His suit was of pale gray serge, his waistcoast a shiny black bib and his collar white, round and without a tie. On his head was a soft black hat and his long hands were thin, graceful and astonishingly white and clean.

Beside him was a woman as short as himself, but plump, with wide apple cheeks, a smiling mouth, hair flecked with gray and a straw hat square on the top of her head. (202)

Reverend Martell and his wife are just the nonthreatening, kindly, protective parents an insecure boy would wish for if he had the chance to make his own choice. In fact, in terms of the novel's imaginative dynamics, Jerome does choose these parents for himself. At the time he requires reassurance and parental care, the Martells appear—not providentially, but called forth by Jerome's need for emotional support and by MacLennan's wish to portray the world as having a benevolent as well as a violent side.

The kindness of the Martells turns Jerome into a devout and basically gentle young man, who "thought of himself as a soldier of God." Catherine reports, "He believed the Gospels literally, and they meant far more to him than they could mean to most people, because he had such a desperate need to belong" (216). However, fighting in the First World War destroys Jerome's religious faith, for the war totally contradicts the rosy picture of the world his foster-parents have taught him to believe in. In his quest for an alternate faith, Jerome becomes a doctor and tries to serve humanity. His search for meaning and goodness takes him first into marriage with Catherine and subsequently into service on the republican side in the Spanish Civil War.

After Jerome is reported dead, George gradually takes over as Catherine's protector; eventually, he becomes her second husband. But supplanting his surrogate father does not complete George's development. George has retained an essential innocence, above all an innocence about himself. He does not want to admit the existence of evil or face the existence of violent emotions within himself. Yet George can attain the inner peace he seeks only after he has recognized and accepted his ambivalent feelings toward the two people who have served him as surrogates for the strong father and mother he never had.

Specifically, George must recognize his suppressed hostility toward both Catherine and Jerome. Just as Jerome makes Harry Blackwell recognize that Harry has really hated Norah for what she did to him, so he also makes George recognize a suppressed side of his character. When George learns that Jerome has been with Catherine in his hospital room, he says he felt "the spirit of murder. I hated them both—Catherine no less than Jerome. I hated myself and I hated life" (306). Catherine's latest illness threatens to destroy George's fragile self-confidence. He is acutely aware of his own inability to help her, and he sees no reason for her suffering. Indeed, he extends Catherine's plight into a paradigm of the human condition:

> The terror is simply this. God, whom we have been taught to regard as a loving Father, appears indifferent. God, whom we have been taught to regard as all-just, is manifestly unconcerned with justice as men understand the meaning of that word. Why should Catherine have to suffer like this? Why should a scoundrel have health and she none? (341–42)

The possibility of Catherine's death, in which he had never really believed before, strips away his veneer of self-assurance: "My maturity had gone and my subconscious had taken over. I was Everyman and every frightened boy and everything and everyone but myself" (339). He is on the verge of giving way to abject self-pity: "'This is destruction!' I heard myself say. 'Of her. Of me because of her. Yes, she has destroyed me. Jerome has destroyed me. Life has destroyed us all. All for nothing. For nothing, for nothing, for nothing!'" (340).

It is Jerome who pulls George back from the brink of mental disintegration. Jerome tells George that Catherine "must be enabled to live her own death." And he says, "You must stop wanting her to die, George" (364). George must come to understand why Catherine holds on to life so tenaciously when further life can only bring her another painful illness. Jerome tells him: "I think what you're afraid of isn't death at all. I think it's life" (366). But Catherine cannot protect George from the ultimate fact of his own mortality. George must recognize that he "married [Catherine] for safety against life" (366). He must learn to fend for himself, not rely totally on the strength of others. Jerome tells him, "You must learn to build a shell around yourself like a snail and every now and then you must creep inside of it" (365). Jerome explains: "The shell is death. You must crawl inside of death and die yourself. You must lose your life. You must lose it to yourself" (365). That is, George must cease to hold an egocentric view of life, in which his own existence is the center of the universe. He must learn that "all loving is loving of life in the midst of death" (69).

In the final stage of his development, George makes Jerome and Catherine his spiritual guides, as they earlier have been his worldly counselors. Both Jerome and Catherine are several times described as "transparent," which seems to indicate that their hold on physical existence has become tenuous and that they live in a realm of the spirit. Both Jerome and Catherine have undergone a kind of rebirth, which Jerome describes to Catherine in the following passage:

"One day I woke up and Jesus himself seemed to be in the cell with me and I wasn't alone. He wasn't anyone I had ever known before. He wasn't the Jesus of the churches. He wasn't the Jesus who died for our sins. He was simply a man who had died and risen again. Who had died outwardly as I had died inwardly."

A little while later he said to Catherine: "You've done that yourself, haven't you?"

"Yes," she said, "more than once." (329-30)

George too must die to himself and be reborn: he must recognize that his own death will not affect the universe of which he is only an infinitesimally small part.

In creating *The Watch That Ends the Night,* MacLennan is attempting to show a character who goes beyond the impasse reached by Dr. Ainslie in *Each Man's Son.* Dr. Ainslie internalized a demanding father; George is trying, through his devotion to Catherine, to internalize a giving mother. Surely George's way holds out more promise of happiness. Moreover, in the final transformation Jerome undergoes in George's eyes, we can see that George has found a way to come to terms with the strong father figure Jerome represents. George says of Jerome:

His whole face seemed transparent. And in his eyes was an expression new and uncanny. They seemed to have seen everything, known everything, suffered everything. But what came out of them into me was light, not darkness. A cool, sweet light came out of them into me then. It entered me, and the murderous feeling went out, and I was not afraid any more. (361)

George no longer perceives the father figure as stern and punitive, but as a forgiving Christ-like redeemer. In this way, Jerome can allay the "Great Fear" in George—the fear of death, the fear of the dark, the fear of one's own insignificance.

It could be argued that George's rapprochement with parental figures is achieved only at a great price, that of the suffering that both Catherine and Jerome undergo. Both parental surrogates undergo a kind of martyrdom, which on the one hand enables George to approach them and on the other hand endows them with a transcendent understanding of life and death. To put matters plainly: it appears that the price of spiritual insight is earthly suffering and physical disfigurement. Jerome assures George that Catherine "must live a little longer in order for you to find out who you are" (364), and the structure of the novel seems to endorse Jerome's statement. George is the main character; the central theme is his confrontation with death and his rejection of a nihilistic despair. That is,

Catherine's illness and Jerome's torture seem to happen only so that George can reach a plateau of understanding he could not otherwise have attained. George ends the novel convinced that the world is meaningful. He also seems to feel that a special providence has arranged events in order to lead him to this insight.

MacLennan has described how, as he worked on *The Watch That Ends the Night,* he discovered that "my intuitions were forcing me to utter something socially blasphemous in those years. They were asserting that God had not been outmoded by the Christian Church, Bertrand Russell, the social scientists, and modern education."[11] In short, MacLennan found himself making a religious statement. George Stewart expresses MacLennan's viewpoint when he says: "I think of this story not as one conditioned by character as the dramatists understand it, but by the spirit. A conflict, if you like, between the spirit and the human condition" (25). Near the end of the novel, George intones MacLennan's final message:

All our lives we had wanted to belong to something larger than ourselves. We belonged consciously to nothing now except to the pattern of our lives and fates. To God, possibly. I am chary of using that much-misused word, but I say honestly that at least I was conscious of His power. Whatever the spirit might be I did not know, but I knew it was there. Life was a gift; I knew that now. And so, much more consciously, did she. (372)

In 1949 MacLennan published in *Maclean's* an article with the accusatory title "Are We a Godless People?"[12] Actually, this title was supplied by the magazine's editors. MacLennan's own title, which he restored when the article was reprinted in *Cross-Country,* was the heartfelt Biblical supplication "Help Thou Mine Unbelief." The article discussed the loss of religious faith that characterized modern society. In the past, man's ultimate purpose had been to serve God. Today, said MacLennan, "a man's goodness is measured—at least in the non-Catholic world—by his material services to his fellow man." This materialistic outlook worried MacLennan, the former student of the decline and fall of the classical world. He insisted, "History reveals clearly that no civilization has long survived after that civilization has lost its religion."

When MacLennan republished "Help Thou Mine Unbelief" in *Cross-Country,* he appended a brief series of afterthoughts. It was tragic, he wrote, "that the Greco-Christian civilization should split into its two original parts, rational humanism and uncritical faith, and that we should be asked to choose between them." He lamented that Western society has opted overwhelmingly for rational thought, with the result that the external universe is viewed as a kind of cosmic machine acting according to the principles of mechanical causality. In this mechanical world, man has no privileged place and as a result feels lost. "This is what I believe to be the essence of the spiritual crisis we face," MacLennan writes. "We are alone and we are purposeless."[13] In *The Watch That Ends the Night,* MacLennan could announce, through George Stewart, that he personally no longer felt alone and purposeless. He was at last "at home" in the world and at peace with himself.

Chapter Six
Psychology and History

Dorothy Duncan's death and his own subsequent remarriage lifted much of the private emotional burden that had made MacLennan turn his thoughts inward during most of the 1950s. Throughout the 1960s, he spoke out vigorously on a number of public issues. He protested against American domination of the magazine-publishing industry in Canada, and he warned against American control of the Canadian economy. He took part in a defense of the literary merits of Lawrence's *Lady Chatterley's Lover* against the censors. Above all, he offered his explanation of the growing unrest that was evident throughout the sixties among the young people of most Western nations.

In short, as the sixties began, MacLennan turned away from the private concerns that had shaped his best writing during the fifties and again wrote as a historically minded observer and as a moralist. Like the essays he published during the 1940s, most of MacLennan's later essays are topical and didactic. They present MacLennan as a concerned citizen speaking out on matters of public importance, rather than as a man of culture and leisure musing in the privacy of his study. This change in outlook is also apparent in the two novels into which, during the sixties and seventies, MacLennan slowly and with much personal anguish poured his feelings about the state of society in the second half of the twentieth century.

Taylor's *Sex in History*

Early in *The Watch That Ends the Night,* George Stewart comments on the difference in outlook between his own prewar generation and the postwar generation whose members fill his university classes:

> These post-war students seemed to me a new breed on earth. They were so much freer in their souls than we had ever been, and so much easier in their emotions. Also, unless the world goes crazy again, they were luckier. For not one of them

could remember the depression or what it had been like when Hitler was the most powerful man in the world. Not one of them was corroded by the knowledge that nobody wanted them.[1]

In several essays written during the 1950s, MacLennan offers a similarly optimistic assessment of the younger generation. For example, he concludes an address given in 1952 by remarking: "This is the best, the clearest-headed, the kindest and the most honest generation Canada has ever had. In many ways, the average Canadian of twenty-one today is more mature than his father and a great deal more so than his grandfather."[2]

In a 1956 article, MacLennan contrasts the current generation of young people with the earlier and very different generation that was raised in Germany during the early years of this century. Coming up in a culture that made a fetish of both self-discipline and obedience to authority, the German young people later "did more harm to humanity and to itself than any group of human beings since Atilla." On the other hand, "the youth of post-war Canada have one dominant ambition. That is to get married and start families as soon as possible. At any rate, they seem to me a pretty stable bunch psychologically."[3]

By the end of the fifties, MacLennan had begun to change his opinion. He was disturbed by an apparent worldwide unrest among the young that gained strength throughout the sixties. Notable acts of student protest took place in Germany, France, and the United States. The protests reached dramatically into Montreal in 1969, when a group of students occupied some of the administrative offices of Sir George Williams University and eventually destroyed many of the university's records and badly damaged its computer facilites. Student unrest was less spectacular at McGill, but MacLennan did witness increasingly vociferous demands for a student voice in deciding on course content and on grading procedures, and heard demands for student representation on the various committees and councils that ran the university.

At the same time, MacLennan observed a growing unrest among the younger Quebecois. MacLennan had welcomed the "Quiet Revolution" fostered by the Lesage government. He thought that an end to domination of Quebec politics by the old alliance between the clergy and the nationalist politicians would at last make Quebec a real part of the modern world, and thereby end the French-Canadian "legend" that had for so long worked to separate Quebec from the rest of Canada. But the Quiet Revolution seemed only to have removed the lid from a seething cauldron of discontent. An aggressive separatist movement soon appeared, and early in the sixties bombs began to explode in Montreal mailboxes.

The coddling of the young by the affluent society had apparently not produced the generation of well-adjusted, security-minded good citizens MacLennan had predicted. MacLennan naturally wondered what had gone wrong. He soon decided he had found the explanation in a book he read in 1960, *Sex in History,* written by the British journalist Gordon Rattray Taylor.[4] Like Freud's later work, *Sex in History* attempts to use psychoanalytic concepts to create a theory of culture. Rather like Erik Erikson's writings, it tries to connect the child-rearing patterns of a particular society with larger cultural patterns.

The best way to summarize MacLennan's understanding of Taylor's ideas is to quote from a newspaper article in which he summarizes the basic thesis of *Sex in History*.[5] Taylor argues, says MacLennan, "that history is made by men, not by God or a dialectic; that men are motivated by their desires; that the pattern of their desires is formed in early childhood. Therefore, if you wish to discover the ultimate source of much political conduct, go to the nurseries where the politicians were nurtured." Taylor contends that "most infants identify themselves, subconsciously, with one or the other of their parents." Those who identify with the father Taylor terms *patrists* and those who identify with the mother are *matrists*. The infant's choice, strongly influenced by cultural patterns, has important consequences. Specifically, patrists are authoritarian in outlook, whereas matrists are permissive. MacLennan explains:

The extreme father-identifier, the "patrist," is compelled by hidden psychological needs to crave authority, and because it is not self-evident that any one man should have authority over others, he develops great skill in persuading himself and mankind that he enjoys a private pipeline to God, or (in the case of Marx) to "the laws of history."

On the other hand, says MacLennan:

The matrist, the mother-identifier, hates conflict and is bored by power. In politics he tends towards democracy, though often he has been content (as in the Renaissance and the late Austrian Empire) to soften by corruption any authoritarian institutions he has inherited.

Patrists, says MacLennan, "despise art, fear luxury, suppress love in themselves and others, and foster learning only in so far as it is useful to their power." In contrast, MacLennan says of matrist societies, "In art and science they are creative, women enjoy an exalted status in them, and in time come to control much of the wealth and (through boudoir politics) the government itself." Neither extreme is desirable in its pure form. Instead, MacLennan argues that "the most brilliant possible period is one in which patrism and matrism exist in balance, as happened in Periclean Athens and Elizabethan England."

Throughout the sixties, MacLennan used Taylor's theories in many speeches and articles, especially when discussing student unrest. He argued that student protest came from a patrist reaction against an excessively matrist society. That is, the students were not anarchists seeking to demolish all rules, but were expressing their frustration at being given no firm standards by their elders. MacLennan also argued that separatist protest, which found its loudest voices among the young, was a patrist reaction against a society widely perceived as decadent and without principles.

By early 1968 MacLennan could claim, as he did in a letter to Edmund Wilson, that he had read Taylor's book four times, each time with greater profit.[6] MacLennan's indebtedness to Taylor's ideas helps to explain important features of his thinking during the sixties and seventies. In particular, MacLennan frequently uses the terms *patrist* and *matrist* in essays and interviews. For example, his retrospective survey of the postwar years, titled "Reflections on Two Decades," relies heavily on Taylor's ideas.[7] MacLennan argues that postwar society has undergone a major transformation, amounting to a revolution. When it took charge of the postwar world, the Depression generation attempted to undo the mistakes of their parents by creating a world of material abundance and permissive social standards. MacLennan says of his generation, "We never deviated in our unconscious aim, which was to recreate the old Victorian patrist world in the image of an indulgent mother wearing pants." His generation were generous toward their children, giving them "what it believed was the greatest of all luxuries, the freedom to choose as adults before they had reached their teens." But the permissive society did not meet the inner need of the young for a coherent structure to their world. The result was the explosion of the sixties, caused by "the trauma of little children who had been cheated of a balanced childhood."

MacLennan, then, is trying to diagnose the failure of the affluent society, which showed "such colossal improvements by matrist standards" but in the end failed to satisfy some of the deepest human needs. He warns:

Our matrist triumph has been purchased at a price which has only recently become apparent. The price has been something mankind has never been able to endure for even a short length of time without becoming hysterical if not destructively insane. That something is the validity of the father, the idea accepted throughout human history that the word "father" implies trust, reliability, a certain valiancy, a deserved authority, and continued respect when he is old.

MacLennan's personal preoccupations are surely influencing this account of society. MacLennan has himself tried to escape the influence of a strong father. He has indirectly attacked Dr. Sam in *Each Man's Son,* and he has turned Dr. Sam into a Christ-like redeemer in *The Watch That Ends the Night.* But now he demonstrates that, although he may give the father a variety of faces, he cannot do without him. There must be a father of some kind, presiding over MacLennan's world as the provider of authority and meaning.

Taylor's theory does not represent a wholly new departure in MacLennan's thinking. Rather, MacLennan found Taylor's book so appealing because it dealt openly with the very patterns that MacLennan's imagination has always been concerned with. MacLennan's novels consistently deal with conflicts between generations and oedipal tensions within the family. Taylor's ideas merely project these conflicts into the larger workings of society. MacLennan found Taylor's ideas very useful in shaping the plots of his next two novels, *Return of the Sphinx* and *Voices in Time.* Specifically, the concept of patrism provided him with a psychological description of the attitude he habitually calls puritanism. Many of MacLennan's writings appear to assume that most of North American society adheres to the same narrow version of Calvinism he knew from his own background. Taylor's ideas gave his account of society a broader basis in a universal theory of human nature.

Return of the Sphinx

In 1962 MacLennan secured a special Canada Council grant and a leave of absence from McGill that enabled him to devote the next winter entirely to work on a new novel. In a farewell message to the readers of a weekly newspaper column he was then writing, he announced with mock humility: "Thanks to the Canada Council I shall once more be a young man with his way to make." Although he did not admit it explicitly, he also divulged the intended subject of his novel when he wrote, "At the moment, it seems to me, the neurosis contingent on the long-delayed silent revolution in Quebec is at a deadlock with a paralysis of will in English-Canada."[8] In *Return of the Sphinx,* MacLennan would examine the forces that were dammed up by this deadlock within confederation. He would also, inevitably, study the larger social disturbances of which developments in Canada were only a part.

MacLennan spent the winter in France, where he tried to improve his French as well as make a start on his novel. His French experiences found their way into the novel in the form of a French character, Gabriel Fleury, whose family home is located in the region near Grenoble where MacLennan spent the winter. However, the novel was not finished until over two years after MacLennan returned home. It appeared in 1967, as though intended by MacLennan as a centennial message to his countrymen. The reviewers, especially in Canada, were not kind to *Return of the Sphinx,* and MacLennan was deeply offended at the apparent rejection of the book he considered "the most dramatic and tightly-written" of all his novels.[9]

MacLennan's opinion notwithstanding, *Return of the Sphinx* vies with *The Precipice* for the dubious honor of being the weakest of his novels. A principal reason for its failure is the reader's difficulty in grasping just what MacLennan is driving at. Peter Buitenhuis, for example, complains that "the reader is often at a loss to understand the motives of the main characters and, in consequence, the thematic ideas of the novel."[10] The difficulty occurs because, although MacLennan sensibly does not use the terms *matrist* and *patrist* in the final draft of *Return of the Sphinx,* the action of the novel is nonetheless shaped to illustrate ideas MacLennan has taken from *Sex in History.* He intended in this novel to deal with what he saw as a worldwide shift in the human psyche, caused by the break-up of a matrist era. Early in the novel, Alan Ainslie tells himself that a "change in the human climate seemed to be occurring everywhere" (72).[11] Although *Return of the Sphinx* has appeared to many readers to be simply an earnest but awkward attempt to warn of the dangers of separatism, it is actually meant to be a psychological novel, not a political treatise in fictional form.

MacLennan wants to show that political events are the outcome of psychological forces created in childhood. Gabriel Fleury, often MacLennan's spokesman in the novel, "had come to the conclusion that all the politics of the world originated in the nurseries of large families like his own or in the despair of outsiders who craved to belong to such groups and didn't" (7). In "Reflections on Two Decades," MacLennan insists, quite rightly, that in *Return of the Sphinx* the "real story was the destruction of a well-meaning father by an unhappy, ambitious, confused, guilt-ridden, idealistic son."[12] The conflict between Alan and Daniel is strongly tinged with sexual rivalry, as the scene in which Alan surprises Daniel with Marielle Jeannotte demonstrates. Daniel mistakenly believes that his sister Chantal has taken her lover Gabriel Fleury into their parents' bed. In emulation, Daniel then takes Marielle into his father's bed, where he is discovered by Alan. Thus, both Daniel and Chantal are involved in sexual relationships that cross the barrier between generations. The difference is that Chantal and Gabriel can cope with the emotional implications of their attraction, whereas Daniel cannot face up to his emotions. Instead, he obtains a bomb from the separatist Aimé Latendresse, and plans to immolate himself in a final gesture of rebellion against the bourgeois society of which his father is a leading member.

Marielle proposes a simple explanation for Daniel's revolutionary politics. She tells him, "You are afraid of loving a woman, and if a man fears that, then it is very natural for him to talk and dream about bombs and war" (153). But it is not MacLennan's intention to argue that separatist politics could be prevented by a generous dose of sexual freedom. Quite the opposite, in fact. Daniel is in fact rebelling against too much freedom. He has been raised in a permissive age, and by a father whose busy career has kept him away from home a great deal. He has grown up without the guidance of any strong authority figure. Daniel, then, is psychologically an orphan, just as Aimé Latendresse is a literal orphan. Both young men are frustrated patrists, deprived of firm standards by the permissiveness of a matrist era.

The society depicted in *Return of the Sphinx* is clearly permissive, or matrist. The loosening of standards in the previously Church-dominated society of Quebec is indicated by the deliberate juxtaposition of images of old and new Quebec in this passage:

When the light halted them at the intersection of Côte des Neiges a covey of black-robed nuns with little white faces peering out of their wimples rustled across in front of them. The nuns were immediately followed by a trio of girls with slovenly hair and the lower halves of their bodies enclosed in skin-tight stretchies, one pink, one magenta, one yellow, and the buttocks of the one in magenta quivered like jello in a mold. (18)

Later in the novel, Daniel Ainslie sees girls "in hip-and-thigh stretchies of thin material and bright colors so that their lines were as clearly drawn as though they were naked" (133). To describe what he sees, he mutters to himself, "Sexacola and Saturday night" (134). These images illustrate

MacLennan's belief that society has entered the brief transitional stage described to Daniel Ainslie by Aimé Latendresse, who "had explained that in the *fin de siècle,* in the trances of desperate pleasure before the cataclysm wipes away an old order, there is always a sexual explosion, a Mardi Gras before another of history's Lenten seasons ushers in the day of retribution and atonement" (134).

In "Reflections on Two Decades," MacLennan explains that the freedom granted to the young has come to be envied by the older generation, who have begun to claim similar pleasures for themselves. The result is a kind of oedipal rivalry between generations in which "the father is beginning to appear as the sexual rival of his son on a scale seldom seen since the Stone Age, while the mother, rejuvenated by the cosmetician, the pharmacist, and a college education, has in cities become a most potent rival of her inexperienced daughter."[13] When Marielle allows Daniel to take her to bed, she intends to release some of his emotional inhibitions, but she is doing exactly the wrong thing: she is yielding when she should be strong, and she is denying the generation gap when she should be insisting on a respectful distance.

Return of the Sphinx may illustrate Taylor's ideas, but as a work of fiction it lacks unity. The novel contains three main lines of action, which are never satisfactorily integrated. The first story the reader encounters is the developing love affair between Gabriel Fleury and Chantal Ainslie. A second story revolves around Alan Ainslie's political troubles in Ottawa. In the wake of a separatist riot, Alan interviews the leaders and promises a bilingual civil service. The resulting controversy in Parliament makes it clear that Alan's solution will not readily achieve political acceptance and may not satisfy Quebec anyway. The third story concerns Daniel Ainslie's brief affair with Marielle and his subsequent plan to place a bomb in a public building. Two of these stories do possess some clear links, for Daniel's involvement in the Montreal riot precipitates Alan's frantic journeying between Ottawa and Montreal; moreover, Alan discovers Daniel acting out his oedipal rivalry, and this confrontation triggers Daniel's decision to plant a bomb; and Daniel's arrest in turn necessitates Alan's resignation from the cabinet. However, the connection of Gabriel and Chantal's love affair to the novel's political themes is not readily apparent.

The outcome of *Return of the Sphinx* is curiously indecisive. By the time the novel ends, Daniel Ainslie and his mentor, the calculating Aimé Latendresse, have been presented as victims of forces they do not understand. The result is to obscure any conventional political thesis that

MacLennan might have seemed to be presenting. The novel appears to be suggesting that there are no clear-cut villains in the modern world, for everyone—good and bad alike—is in the grip of powerful external forces. Indeed, the theme of man's inability to control his world pervades the novel. The death of Alan's wife Constance took place "by chance"; Gabriel Fleury reflects, "People still talked about the senselessness of that accident" (61). Alan Ainslie sees his whole generation as controlled by external forces. He asks himself:

> Could Daniel ever, ever understand how it had been for men of his age? How events had happened to so many of them and how some, like himself, had been driven to do irrevocable things not out of any fate created by their characters—at least so far as he understood his own character—but because such things had come with the rations of the epoch into which they had been born. (115)

Even with several careers behind him—as a university teacher, a diplomat, a bomber pilot, a magazine editor—Alan Ainslie "still felt a failure, still felt a young man with his way to make" (116). At the height of his uncertainty, when he cannot find his children despite his trip to Montreal, Alan reaches the bleak conclusion "that nothing he could think, say or do could be of the least significance to anyone" (165).

The basic theme of the novel is Alan Ainslie's search for a way out of this emotional dead end. Events give him little help. His well-meant gesture of talking to the young separatists is not understood in English Canada. His own son turns out to be a separatist. His political ideas are politely shunted aside by Bulstrode's announcement that the government will create yet another Royal Commission to study the problem of French-English relations in Canada. Nevertheless, in the final paragraph of the novel, Alan Ainslie reaches an inner peace very like that attained by George Stewart at the end of *The Watch That Ends the Night*:

> Looking over the lake he at last accepted that he had merely happened into all this. Constance, Chantal, Daniel, Gabriel—they and all the others had merely happened into this loveliness that nobody could understand or possess, and that some tried to control or destroy just because they were unable to possess or understand it. Merely happened into this joy and pain and movement of limbs, of hope, fear, shame and the rest of it, the little chipmunk triumphs and defeats. He believed it would endure. He thanked God he had been of it, was of it. (303)

The affirmative spirit of this conclusion seems inconsistent with the action that precedes it. On the surface, Alan Ainslie's story is a tragedy. He fails to re-establish communication with his son; in fact, his son brings about the end of his political career. All that separates Ainslie's final acceptance of the world from a period when he "went through the mechanisms of a man in a state of partial amnesia" (297) is a series of journeys throughout Canada. The therapeutic qualities of Alan's travels are not dramatized. MacLennan's confidence in the land as a restorer of health comes from his own experience, for he made a similar series of journeys shortly after his wife died and he completed *The Watch That Ends the Night*. But in *Return of the Sphinx*, Alan's restoration by contact with the land seems arbitarily imposed by the author.

At bottom, MacLennan's outlook in *Return of the Sphinx*, like his outlook in *The Watch That Ends the Night*, is religious. During the early sixties, he publicly referred to himself as a "lapsed Presbyterian,"[14] a condition he seems to share with Alan Ainslie, who tells his children that he believes in God but won't go to church (42). Instead of worshipping privately, Alan tries to put his ideals into practice in the social and political world. Thus, MacLennan's own inner debate between a contemplative and an activist stance to the world is reflected in the novel by the difference in outlook between Alan Ainslie and Gabriel Fleury. Gabriel Fleury represents MacLennan's contemplative and private side, the part of his mind that is skeptical about the motives of politicians and dubious that any individual can change the world. As Joe Lacombe says of Gabriel: "That Frenchman worries too much. He makes a science of it. No matter what it is about something, you talk to old Gabriel for five minutes and it's so complicated you don't know where you are" (88). On the other hand, Alan Ainslie has always impetuously committed himself to an idealistic attempt to bring about change. In trying to save Canada, Alan is acting out the teachings of his foster-father, the Dr. Ainslie portrayed in *Each Man's Son*. Dr. Ainslie gave his adopted son, as Chantal Ainslie puts it, "the idea that his life ought to be some kind of Pilgrim's Progress to some kind of City of God" (43). In portraying Alan Ainslie's attempts to realize his foster-father's ideals, MacLennan is expressing the side of his own nature that adhered to the values of classical humanism and from time to time spoke publicly in their defense.

At first sight it may seem farfetched to consider *Return of the Sphinx* a personal, almost autobiographical, statement on MacLennan's part. MacLennan has never held political office or been known as a participant in party politics. On the surface, none of Alan Ainslie's accomplishments as diplomat, war hero, magazine editor, or politician mark him as an obvious alter ego for MacLennan. Nonetheless, resemblances to MacLennan do exist. When the novel begins, Alan has recently lost his wife in a "senseless" manner, as did MacLennan when Dorothy Duncan died. The aims of Ainslie's and MacLennan's careers coincide in many ways. Ainslie has devoted his most strenuous efforts to fostering a stronger sense of Candian nationalism through better understanding between the two founding peoples. He has twice sacrificed a promising diplomatic career to act on his principles: once when he enlisted in the air force, although technically overage, and again when he founded a magazine of political comment. MacLennan, too, has devoted much of his career to fostering a stronger sense of Canadian identity and to encouraging Canada's two founding peoples to cooperate in order to defeat the political colossus to the south. Yet in *Return of the Sphinx,* Alan Ainslie's journalistic and political efforts seem to accomplish very little. Is MacLennan here asking, in an indirect way, whether his own literary career has been effective? When the novel ends with Alan's renewed expression of faith in the meaning of life, the reader recognizes that this book can be viewed as an extended apologia in fictional form for MacLennan's own career.

In fact, like MacLennan, Alan Ainslie is an author. He has written an autobiographical memoir titled *Death of a Victorian.* The full significance of the title only becomes apparent when Alan speaks about his fosterfather, Dr. Ainslie. "Dr. Ainslie believed that education could cure everything," he says. "He was a Victorian, of course, and all the Victorians believed that" (239). Alan Ainslie too once believed that education —by fostering reason, knowledge, self-examination, discussion, and compromise—could solve Canada's problems and eventually solve the problems of the modern world. This is the belief that Alan Ainslie terms Victorian, and *Return of the Sphinx* might itself have been titled *Death of a Victorian.* Alan Ainslie seeks desperately to steer himself and his country into a safe harbor; in a world from which all certainty seems to have vanished, he tries to believe there is a meaningful pattern behind events. In his perplexity and in his nostalgia for a vanished age of faith, Alan resembles his creator, Hugh MacLennan.

The "death" in the title *Death of a Victorian* refers to the loss of faith in those ideas that once seemed the bedrock of civilization. The death of Victorianism, then, means the end of an easy optimism in one's outlook on life. Alan Ainslie tells an uncomprehending House of Commons, "I believe the crisis came when humanity lost its faith in man's ability to improve his own nature" (267). Ainslie, like MacLennan himself, has a fundamentally conservative outlook on human nature. He believes that virtue is difficult to attain and must be taught by education and by example. Therefore, to lose faith in the effectiveness of education is to lose faith that morality can be made to govern human conduct.

MacLennan was particularly sensitive to adverse criticism of *Return of the Sphinx* because, in important ways, he had made a heavy emotional investment in the novel. *The Watch That Ends the Night* was obviously confessional to the extent that Catherine's story was based on Dorothy Duncan's fate. *Return of the Sphinx* is a personal novel in a more indirect way. MacLennan attributes many of his most deeply held values to Alan Ainslie, so that Ainslie expresses MacLennan's own fear that his most cherished values are doomed in the modern world. In a letter written in 1970 to the critic Robert Cockburn, MacLennan claimed that he knew many people who, like Alan Ainslie, had unselfishly sacrificed their personal lives for the good of their country. But his assessment of their impact is pessimistic:

> I don't think they will be able to save us from the States—which is no longer a nation but the base of a military-corporation-international structure rapidly becoming as barbarous as the ROMAN Empire. But it does seem to me that the essence of man's fate today is the dying struggle of the brave and able individual against the forces of disintegration inherent in technology.[15]

This passage can serve as a gloss on Alan Ainslie's career in *Return of the Sphinx*. It can also stand as an accurate account of the way MacLennan saw his own career during these years.

Yet *Return of the Sphinx* concludes, however unconvincingly, on an affirmative note. Unlike Athanase Tallard, who also tried to straddle the gap between French and English in Canada, Alan does not let the antagonism of the two opposing "legends" destroy his personality. Like Athanase, Alan is attacked by a bitter and guilt-ridden son; and like his foster-father, Alan drives himself to meet the exacting standards set by a strict and demanding father. But unlike Athanase and unlike Dr. Ainslie, Alan can rise above the destructive emotions that his personal situation threatens to create.

Return of the Sphinx ends with a neat reversal of the explosive oedipal confrontation that turns up at the climax of many of MacLennan's novels. Alan Ainslie discovers his son Daniel in circumstances that clearly indicate the son's desire to supplant the father. The reader may well expect a final outbreak of onstage violence to close dramatically a novel that has already told of a series of violent deaths in the past. Alan Ainslie, the reader may remember, witnessed his mother's death at his father's hands; Bulstrode saw his parents die; Marielle saw her father's warship blown up; and Constance Ainslie was crushed by a runaway truck. In fact, Alan's first impulse upon discovering Daniel and Marielle is a violent one:

> Something snapped in Ainslie and he leaped at Daniel with his fists clenched and raised. Daniel, hands at his sides, eyes horrified, awaited him motionless. Ainslie's fist moved and in his brain was a flash of light and a silent voice shouting, "Not you too—no, not you—for God's sake not you too!" and his fist stopped in mid-air as the muscles refused to drive it. His hands loosened and fell to his sides like weights. His shoulders sagged and he turned to go back to his study.
> "Get out," he said quietly, "both of you." (286)

Alan checks himself in time; he does not re-enact his natural father's violent deed. He feels a murderous impulse, but he recognizes and controls it. Moreover, Alan subsequently sanctions Chantal's generation-spanning alliance with Gabriel Fleury. In effect, Alan is admitting that oedipal desires are inevitable and should be no source of guilt.

George Stewart and Alan Ainslie both claim to have resolved for themselves one of the most insistent problems treated in MacLennan's fiction: the need to feel there is a meaningful pattern behind the random appearance of events. Artistically, *The Watch That Ends the Night* presents this resolution more attractively, for it blends theme and technique more harmoniously than any other of MacLennan's novels. But perhaps the story of Alan Ainslie does carry the quest for self-assurance one step beyond the stopping place reached by George Stewart. Alan Ainslie remains malleable into middle age and remains ready to confront new and potentially disturbing experiences. The reader feels that Alan will remain engaged with the world around him, the world of political events and other people, rather than taking refuge in the quietism that consoles George Stewart.

The Risen Animal

MacLennan has said, "Of the stuff I've written, the one that ripped out my guts the most was *Return of the Sphinx*."[16] The effort of charting what he later called "the crack in the human psyche" that opened as society underwent one of its periodic shifts between patrism and matrism left him emotionally and intellectually exhausted. "To be a novelist during these years," MacLennan explains, "was to be in extra-sensory perception with apparent chaos. By the time the decade ended, I knew I must pause for a new perspective."[17] One of the projects with which MacLennan diverted himself during his holiday from fiction was the preparation of an expanded version of his 1961 book *Seven Rivers of Canada*. In the introduction to the new book, published as *Rivers of Canada,* MacLennan describes how preparing the earlier version had been a welcome relief after the strain of writing *The Watch That Ends the Night*. But the new book "meant far more to my soul and sanity than its simpler and much shorter predecessor possibly could" (7). For, as he traveled the country preparing the new book, he discovered the "new perspective" he needed in order to return to the writing of fiction.

MacLennan turned away from the society in turmoil he had depicted in *Return of the Sphinx*. "I wanted to try to think like a river," he says, "even though a river doesn't think. Because every river on this earth, some of them against incredible obstacles, ultimately finds its way through the labyrinth to the universal sea" (8). MacLennan's researches forced him to think not only about Canada's recorded history but also about the geological past of the regions through which the nation's rivers flow. He came to think of the natural world in what was for him a new way: he came to see it as a living organism. In other words, he learned that slow but inevitable changes take place in the natural world as well as in human societies.

Prompted in addition by the "new biology" popularized by writers such as Robert Ardrey and Desmond Morris, MacLennan realized that mankind is a participant in the larger evolutionary process, not a species set apart from nature. This outlook gave him a new perspective on the troubled sixties. The strife of these years was not necessarily a catastrophe, but could be interpreted as evidence that society was undergoing a speeded-up evolutionary change. "It was the fate of my generation," MacLennan remarks, "to have been born in the death-throes of a civilization that had supported the West for nearly two thousand years" (11). Yet MacLennan found reason for hope. He suggested that the present young generation "had not been educated to be ashamed of their own humanity. They did not believe that man is a fallen creature" (11). Rather, the new generation instinctively saw themselves as part of nature. They knew that "man is not a fallen innocent but a risen animal. In spite of his follies and crimes, on the balance he has more reason for pride than for shame" (11). In effect, MacLennan is expressing his hope that in the new generation the "ancient curse" of self-destructive guilt has at last been permanently lifted.

In the epilogue to *Rivers of Canada,* MacLennan describes how he watched with horror as downtown Montreal was razed and rebuilt into "slab-buildings, egg-crate buildings, wall-buildings, works of architecture inspired by Hitler's bunker and maximum-security jails" (266). But he does not succumb to despair. Instead he looks to the new generation to tear down the urban monstrosities and reassert man's need to live in harmony with the natural environment. He envisions a gentler future: "The St. Lawrence would still be there when the human race recovered from its present madness. . . . There would be no more land speculators and the people living in the river-city would enjoy it again" (12). The destruction of the Montreal MacLennan had come to know so well undoubtedly helped him to imagine the holocaust that destroys most of modern civilization in *Voices in Time*. But in the world of MacLennan's latest novel, the St. Lawrence is again unpolluted and salmon can be caught from the shores of Montreal Island.

Voices in Time

Voices in Time is MacLennan's most ambitious attempt to chart the troubled course of public events in our time. Into this novel MacLennan has distilled his impassioned responses to a terrifying century. As a result, the novel contains both too much and too little. *Voices in Time* bulges untidily with incidents and characters; even more obviously, it bulges with MacLennan's theorizing about the forces shaping modern history. But too little is done with this material; the novel's characters are shallowly drawn and their actions are a schematic illustration of a preconceived intellectual position. In the end, *Voices in Time* takes its place with *The Precipice* and *Return of the Sphinx* as one of MacLennan's failures, a thesis novel rather than a novel of character. It exhibits most of MacLennan's weaknesses and few of his virtues as a novelist.

In *Return of the Sphinx*, MacLennan intended to deal with a universal crisis facing twentieth-century society, not just with a parochial Canadian political question. But he set his novel in the Montreal of the sixties, where the French-English conflict in Canada was most acute, and he stressed the conflict between the staunch federalist Alan Ainslie and his separatist son. Unwisely, too, he left it largely to the past histories of Alan Ainslie and Gabriel Fleury to indicate his larger concerns. In *Voices in Time,* he wants to forestall any possibility that readers may fail to comprehend his meaning. Therefore, the events of his plot span more than a hundred years, and he presents many lengthy passages in which the characters analyze in detail the significance of the events in which they are involved. In short, the historian's impulse to diagnose society's ills and explain its workings wins out over the novelist's impulse to follow the fortunes of specific characters in particular situations. In *Voices in Time,* the ideas overwhelm what is, at a personal level, yet another of MacLennan's stories of corrosive hostility between fathers and sons.

The characters of *Voices in Time* enact, as did the characters of *Return of the Sphinx,* a charade whose meaning is derived from Taylor's *Sex in History.* Timothy Wellfleet rails against the decadent standards of his overly permissive, or matrist, society when he asks:

> How could anyone be a human being in that decade of the spiritual *castrati,* programmed by Dr. Spock, interpreted by the interpreters of Dr. Freud, its religion packaged in cellophane by Doctors Peale, Sheen and Graham, the whole lot of them conned into believing, into really believing, that nobody in the history of this world had had it so good as us?[18]

The historian Conrad Dehemel corroborates Timothy's judgment when he explains why he fears that the sixties will give rise to a new social upheaval. "The entire world is screaming for freedom and is sincere about it," he writes, "but they don't understand what freedom is. The most violent screamers are really screaming for release from freedom's discipline, which means they are screaming for somebody to return them to slavery" (295).

Conrad Dehemel and Timothy Wellfleet are MacLennan's two principal case histories. Dehemel's story shows the helplessness of a good man caught up in the currents of violence and persecution that swept the world in the thirties and forties. Timothy Wellfleet's story shows the moral and spiritual bankruptcy that can overwhelm a child of the mid-century affluent society. Dehemel grows up in an excessively patrist society; in later life he becomes a victim of the incipient patrist reaction against the matrist era that emerged after the Second World War. Timothy Wellfleet is a product of a matrist society that is ripe for takeover by a new wave of authoritarian repression.

In this novel, MacLennan hides himself behind two masks. One is the aging, reflective narrator, John Wellfleet, who is only a little older than was MacLennan himself at the time he wrote the novel. John Wellfleet shares MacLennan's fondness for lilacs, and his face resembles MacLennan's, complete with the same "loose gray hair receding from a high, rectangular forehead with a prominent vein on the left side" (21). Most importantly, John Wellfleet's struggles to piece together the story told in the documents André Gervais has provided reflects MacLennan's own concern to interpret the meaning of the past to a generation that has almost completely lost its historical memory. MacLennan's other alter ego is the German historian Conrad Dehemel, who—like MacLennan's earlier "young men of 1933"—is caught up in events he cannot control. Moreover, he has written a thesis based on the same papyrus documents that MacLennan once studied at Princeton, and like MacLennan's dissertation, Dehemel's study highlights the parallels between life in the later years of the Roman Empire and life in the twentieth century. Above all, Dehemel's inability to fight the historical forces that warp his life and separate him from his fiancée, Hanna Erlich, mirrors MacLennan's own sense of being battered by external forces for much of his life.

The main action of *Voices in Time* takes place in the middle years of the twentieth century. But this action is recounted from the temporal perspective of the fourth decade of the twenty-first century. The principal viewpoint is that of John Wellfleet, seventy-five years old when the novel begins, a survivor of "The Great Fear" and "the Destructions" that destroyed most of the civilization we know today. André Gervais, a young man interested in the past, recovers some papers written by members of John Wellfleet's family and asks Wellfleet to use them as the basis for a book that would clarify the past for members of the historically innocent new generation.

Voices in Time is structured as a collage of several narrative lines, and it is largely a book of memories, somewhat in the manner of *The Watch That Ends the Night*. The memories belong, however, not to the narrator but to several other people—really to society as a whole. As John Wellfleet sifts through the stories of Conrad Dehemel and Timothy Wellfleet, his reactions capture the process of trying to understand a confused and violent past. But perhaps the best way to explain the meaning of *Voices in Time* is not to follow the sequence in which events are told in the book, but to present events in their historical order as John Wellfleet will finally unravel them for André Gervais.

Conrad Dehemel's story begins in the years before the First World War. By describing Conrad's father, an officer in the German Navy, MacLennan shows the mentality that led Germany into the war. Then he examines the way the same authoritarian mentality refused to learn from the defeat and instead set about preparing for another armed confrontation. Conrad Dehemel endorses none of the values that animate the German ruling class, but he nonetheless finds himself powerless to prevent the takeover by the Nazis, and he finds that his own private life is invaded by the evil that Hitler has unleashed.

Conrad's father is a loyal and obedient officer. He is, says Conrad, a good man in his way. But he is scrupulously obedient to authority and has implicit faith in traditional German values. He belongs to a generation that "with absolute courage did what they thought was their duty and thereby became the most destructive generation the world has ever known" (136). The defeat of the German Navy, and especially the rebellion of seamen against their officers, shocks Conrad's father. But he learns nothing from these events. He can only insist that next time Germany will not make the same mistakes. As Conrad's grandfather says of Germans in general: "When the orders are given, yes, they will obey them again. They have learned nothing and they will forget nothing" (152).

Conrad's father is the epitome of his society. "He was an educated man," Conrad tells us, "far from insensitive, who loved art and music. His discipline was awesome and it was bolted to the only things he had been trained to value—his service, his country, and whoever might become his wife" (135). His belief in the conventional wisdom prevents him from ever really knowing himself: "He would still believe that he loved his wife and might even believe that he loved me, but his true home had never been any house or apartment where Mother and I might live. It had been his profession and now his profession was gone. Now he was an officer with no men to command, a sailor with no navy to serve" (157). Conrad's father retreats into a private world and lives only for the time when a rebuilt navy will vindicate his country's honor.

Conrad's mother, on the other hand, does not conform to the usual pattern of German womanhood: "Most of them had been trained to think of themselves as Roman matrons and the war made some of them much fiercer than the men to whom they were supposed to be subservient" (140). Conrad's mother "loathed war" and communicated her gentleness to her son. It is her influence, together with the teachings and example of a kindly grandfather, that instill more liberal values into young Conrad and keep him emotionally and intellectually flexible.

Conrad starts a promising career as a historian. Yet his real motivation is "to release himself from his father without making his father despise him" (180). Before his career is properly under way, however, he is swept into the maelstrom of Nazi racism. He returns to Germany to study under the renowned art historian, Professor Rosenberg. But Rosenberg is summarily dismissed for being a Jew, and Conrad unexpectedly finds himself made director of the institute. Later, as part of a plan to help his Jewish fiancée and her father, he becomes part of the German Naval Intelligence Service and later still he enlists in the Gestapo. As part of his training, he must witness the torture of several prisoners. Thus, for the most honorable of motives, Conrad becomes morally implicated in the worst features of the Nazi "final solution." Even a "good German" like Conrad Dehemel cannot escape the contamination Hitler's psychosis has brought to his people. Conrad's facial resemblance to a notoriously cruel Gestapo officer not only precipitates his murder but also symbolically underlines his moral involvement in whatever his nation has done.

Throughout this story, the arch-villain, Hitler, remains offstage. Instead, he is diagnosed in clinical Freudian terms by Dr. Erlich, Hanna Erlich's father, who is a psychiatrist. Dr. Erlich explains that in Hitler the authoritarian German superego, or conscience, "has combined with a particularly ferocious and cruel id to crush out his original ego as though it had been caught between a hammer and an anvil. Adolph Hitler the little corporal? Adolph Hitler the dreamer and failed artist? That man has literally ceased to exist and an entirely different man has been born" (176). The transformed Hitler is now the very personification of the German neurosis. After the 1929 collapse, millions of Germans were out of work, and, says Dr. Erlich, "a German out of work feels sick in his mind" (174). Therefore, Dr. Erlich explains, "Most people in Germany have been made to feel like nobodies. The young believe that nobody wants them" (175). Hitler offers them a chance to become somebodies; he provides redemption from the despair that makes Adolph Fabricius attempt suicide in MacLennan's unpublished novel "So All Their Praises." Hitler acts as the superego of his people, assuring them that what they are doing is right.

In contrast to Hitler and the Nazis, the family of Hanna Erlich represent European civilization at its best. Although each of the Erlich men has a career or profession, they all "assumed that the ultimately important things were art, science, music, and literature" (173). John Wellfleet, voicing MacLennan's opinion, enviously remarks: "The Erlichs were entwined with a long European experience going back into the past for centuries. My continent, the democratic continent, never had known anything comparable" (171–72). But the Erlich family's belief in culture prevents them from recognizing the sinister motives behind Hitler's maneuvers until it is too late. As John Wellfleet explains, "Trained men of reason are the last to recognize the bared teeth of the human ape when it appears before them. Half a century later, when I was young, it was the same story all over again" (178).

Postwar North America is demoralized for different reasons than was Depression Germany, but demoralized it is. In fact, the later era is the obverse of the earlier one. Hitler's Germany was a patrist culture; mid-century North America is a matrist society. Germany tried to impose its will on the world; its frustration threshold was too low to brook any opposition to its wishes. Mid-century North America abandons all social restraints; it imposes no standards, but simply caters to the ever-rising level of material expectations among its citizens. Timothy Wellfleet speaks scornfully of the way the "system" buys off young people with the modern equivalents of Roman bread and circuses.

Timothy Wellfleet is himself a representative member of his society, the virtual embodiment of his era. He works for a time among the high priests of consumerism in an advertising agency. Then he becomes a television personality whose intuitions are open to the undercurrents of the society around him, so that he can say: "The world was not my stage. I was the stage for the world" (97). On his television show, he is the sort of aggressive interviewer who belittles or entraps his guests and makes himself the focus of attention. His brand of radical chic requires that he efface himself only when he gives exposure to critics of the established order and that he attack all guests who represent the establishment. When it turns out that his program has featured several of the separatists who are responsible for the kidnappings that trigger Canada's October Crisis, the producer of the show, who is Jewish, accuses Timothy of encouraging terrorism. She laments, "My family came to this country to get rid of political maniacs and now it's beginning to look like the same story all over again" (60).

Timothy Wellfleet is one of MacLennan's resentful sons, like Marius Tallard and Daniel Ainslie. He despises both his parents and is exposed only briefly to surrogate parental figures he can respect (his maternal grandfather and John Wellfleet's mother). When it is too late, Timothy realizes that his father is a man of honor. But the damage is done, for the father has misguidedly indulged Timothy when he should have imposed limits. "Why could he never understand," Timothy complains, "that the last thing I needed from him was any kind of indulgence and the one thing I inwardly craved was the kind of leadership he had given his men at Walcheren?" (43). Such permissive behavior is not natural to Timothy's father, a career soldier. He is simply conforming to postwar social expectations and in the process dying "from spiritual malnutrition." Timothy says, "Of course, on the surface he was a success story, which meant he was a classic failure story" (41).

MacLennan makes it clear that Timothy's pseudoradical politics are an expression of his troubled personal life. Timothy, the resentful son, attacks the representatives of the established order, whom he sees as restrictive parental figures. Overtly, he rebels against restrictive social standards, but if he could only admit it, he would prefer that a genuinely orderly society be re-established. Knowing that he lacks inner standards himself, Timothy seeks to tear down those who seem to possess fixed standards. He cannot bear to meet men of real integrity—men therefore better than himself. Knowing his own degradation, he must try to show that others are equally debased.

MacLennan uses Timothy's neurotic obsession with sex to indicate his overall moral bankruptcy. A crude sexuality pervades all aspects of Timothy's life. The title of his television show, *This Is Now*, is given to him by the orgasmic outcry of his mistress; his sensational approach to journalism resembles a publicly conducted encounter therapy session. Timothy thinks of his show as an attempt to "mate with their [the viewers'] hidden fears and truths" (72). The puerile sexual level of his show is set by an interview with a female poet, whose subject matter is sexual love and whose mission is to utter the magic word *fuck* over the airwaves of the publicly financed CBC.

It may seem that both Hitler and Timothy Wellfleet are being explained away as merely the inevitable outcome of a particular set of psychological stresses. But psychological determinism is not the novel's final position. Conrad Dehemel remarks: "Dr. Erlich explained why Hitler became a psychotic. But as time passes I'm not sure even he explained how it was possible for a man like Hitler to become our master" (294). A more comprehensive explanation is given by Dehemel himself, when he tells Timothy during their televised interview:

"Everyone knows the political and economic explanation, but the deeper cause is often ignored. . . . After the 1914 war, religion died out among millions of young Germans. This left a void in their lives and many turned to nationalism as a substitute for the religion they had lost. In the 1960s, religion also died out among the young all over the world and nationalisms of every kind are taking its place." (115)

This is really the didactic heart of MacLennan's novel. Dehemel's assessment closely echoes George Stewart's conclusion in *The Watch That Ends the Night* that his own generation desperately sought substitutes for the religion they thought they had outgrown; they did not realize that their hunger for meaning made them easy pickings for the cynical manipulations of power-hungry men.

The narrator of *Voices in Time*, John Wellfleet, is also a child of the sixties. He tells André Gervais, "For a time I was hooked on hash—that was a drug we smoked. I had no ambition and I used to wander around the world" (26). Unfortunately, John Wellfleet is just not very interesting as a character. He tells us that he has had one genuine love in his life, but he doesn't describe this romance. He is simply a narrative device by which MacLennan tries to impose unity on the stories of two different men and two different historical eras. Cameron argues that his attempt to assemble a meaningful pattern out of scattered facts and scraps of personal memory is an effective presentation of the artist's creation of order out of the chaos of experience.[19] But, though we are told that John Wellfleet works from fragmentary evidence, we never see him grapple with the elusiveness of historical truth. The novel impresses the reader as being based on a confidently held theory of history. If John Wellfleet serves a purpose, it is to guide the reader's response to the stories of Conrad and Timothy. In short, he is simply a conventional omniscient narrator, masquerading as a fallible character in MacLennan's fictional world.

John Wellfleet reports that a conservative backlash to the hedonistic but empty existence of the sixties and seventies soon took place. It was triggered by the series of events Wellfleet terms the "Great Fear," in which highly organized international gangs held governments to ransom by threatening to set off nuclear explosions in major population centers. This spectacle of apparent anarchy brought to the surface all the resentment felt by those who had been a bit too old or too inhibited to join in the frolic enjoyed by John Wellfleet's generation. The result is a wave of repression directed against the free-living young:

> These unknown millions we had dismissed as red-necks felt against us a rage deeper than anything they had felt against the bombers. Furious voices spewed out hatred and loathing against my whole generation. *We* were the spoiled brats who had been responsible for all their woes. *We* were the ones who had destroyed their authority over their children and foisted our own laziness and sensuality onto everyone else. (244)

Though on a larger scale, this reaction expresses feelings that are actually similar to Timothy's unacknowledged longing for a more authoritative father. In response, an authoritarian government does take over, which John Wellfleet calls the Second Bureaucracy. Apparent stability returns to society, for "the Great Fear abated now that the mass of the people believed they were under an authority strong enough to rule them" (246).

The Second Bureaucracy's control is illusory, however, for shortly thereafter the worst nightmare of a nuclear society comes to pass. The computers of the rival bureaucracies, John Wellfleet theorizes, "suffered the equivalent of a collective nervous breakdown" (247). The survivors, under the strict control of the Third Bureaucracy, eventually begin to re-establish an ordered society. All knowledge about the past is rigidly controlled, and a simplified version of history known as the Diagram is taught in the schools. It is this mass historical amnesia that André Gervais asks John Wellfleet to repair.

Wellfleet is trying to answer a question asked by André Gervais: "If there were men like him [Conrad Dehemel] with all that knowledge, why couldn't they stop what happened?" (121). John Wellfleet faces a limited—though difficult enough—task: he must make sense of events that are known to have happened. MacLennan's own purpose is surely more ambitious still. He wishes not just to describe a disaster that is already part of history but to avert a catastrophe that has not yet happened. Through Conrad Dehemel's story, MacLennan revisits the Hitler era in order to display the forces that allowed Hitler's madness to be unleashed on the world. Then, through Timothy Wellfleet's story, he makes the surprising assertion that the same forces that operated in Hitler's Germany are at work in mid-century North America. Finally, through John Wellfleet's story, MacLennan warns his readers that the possibility of a holocaust worse than Hitler's hangs over today's society.

Like Freud, MacLennan has reservations about the long-term success of mankind's experiment in sublimation. Yet the mood of *Voices in Time* is not one of unrelieved gloom. MacLennan's cyclical view of history allows him to see the social catastrophes he describes as only passing phases in a continuing process. At the end of the novel, society is renewing itself through the efforts of young men such as André Gervais. At the beginning of his task of historical reconstruction, John Wellfleet writes: "As it is with the individual, so it may be with the whole world. When the individual is wounded in his soul he often wishes to die. But time passes and then, for no reason he understands, he wants to live again. Can it be the same with communities?" (28). This note of cautious optimism could well express MacLennan's own mood as he brings to a close his most exhaustive fictional survey of North American society. MacLennan hopes his book offers a timely warning that will forestall in life the catastrophe that befalls his fictional world. If he succeeds, he will have raised his own voice "in time." He will have spoken soon enough to prevent a tragedy.

Stated this bluntly, MacLennan's aim is grandiose to the point of absurdity or arrogance. MacLennan seems to have forgotten a truth about fiction that he expressed in print at about the time he was beginning to write *Voices in Time:* "I have long ago learned that it is impossible to persuade anyone to change his attitudes by telling him to change them. Conrad was right when he said that the writer's task is to make you hear, to make you feel, above all to make you see."[20] But in *Voices in Time,* MacLennan ignores his own warning. His novel simply does not succeed as fiction, whereas the more sensitively developed story in George Orwell's *Nineteen Eighty-Four,* which is also set in a bleak future society, does succeed. *Voices in Time* is an atypical work of Canadian fiction. Its closest precedent in Canadian literature is probably Frederick Philip Grove's *The Master of the Mill.* Like Grove's novel, *Voices in Time* is an ambitious attempt, undertaken by an earnest and sometimes ponderously didactic author, to define the principal forces shaping twentieth-century society. And in MacLennan's novel, as in Grove's, the message takes precedence over the story, much to the detriment of the book's final effectiveness.

With his latest novel, MacLennan's career has come full circle. *Voices in Time* returns to the prewar political situation that was the subject of his two early unpublished novels and deals with a topic—the decay of an entire civilization—that was the subject of MacLennan's doctoral dissertation. In the fullness of age, MacLennan seems to have become determined to finish the book his younger self had twice tried to write. Through the persona of John Wellfleet, MacLennan reviews the succession of calamities that he sees making up twentieth-century history. But he is no longer an insecure social outcast, no longer a "young man of 1933." As a result, the bitterness and the self-pity found in the earlier novels are gone. John Wellfleet does not demand sympathy for himself and does not try to condemn the people whose stories he tells. Instead, he tries to understand them—and so inevitably to forgive them their mistakes and meannesses. John Wellfleet is saddened by his survey of the folly of mankind, but he is not broken in spirit. He can still respond to the return of the birds, to the flowering of the lilacs, and to the birth of André Gervais's daughter. As MacLennan himself can still respond to such things.

Chapter Seven
Man of Letters

Hugh MacLennan has presented himself to the Canadian public in an impressive variety of literary roles: as a novelist, a familiar essayist, a travel writer, a political analyst, and an occasional reviewer and critic. As George Woodcock points out, "More than most Canadian writers MacLennan [has] approximated to the European type of *homme de lettres* who writes . . . in a variety of genres without creating a hierarchy of values" among his writings.[1] In everything he has written, MacLennan has expounded his personal vision of Canada and has defended traditional values that he feels are endangered in the modern world. His writings possess a unity of outlook that makes his career more than the mere sum of its parts.

Novelist

MacLennan has made his greatest contribution to Canadian letters through his novels. He belongs to a generation of Canadian writers whose other leading members are Ethel Wilson, Morley Callaghan, Ernest Buckler, Sinclair Ross, W. O. Mitchell, and Robertson Davies. (The enigmatic Frederick Philip Grove, though somewhat older, might also be included as a kind of ex officio member of this group.) Except for Ethel Wilson, these writers came to maturity during the late twenties and early thirties. Their lives and careers were shadowed by the fall from the Jazz Age into the Depression. As a group, their major contribution was to reverse the emphasis on romance and local color that prevailed in Canadian fiction until well into the twentieth century. With the exception of Callaghan, all began publishing books at a relatively late age and experienced difficulty in making a literary career into a paying proposition. Thus, they exemplify the marginal status so often allotted to the artist in Canadian society.

Writers of this generation brought about an important change in the Canadian literary climate. In 1941 MacLennan asserted that there was no tradition of Canadian literature. By 1959, when *The Watch That Ends the Night* was published, he could write to the German critic Paul Goetsch that he "felt at least as free in his Canadian milieu as any American or Englishman in his."[2] MacLennan's comment draws attention to the swiftness with with Canadian literature developed during the forties and fifties. MacLennan's own contribution to this process was crucial. By combining high public visibility with a serious purpose, he made Canadian literature both widely known and respectable. To no small degree, the confidence with which many later writers have embarked on literary careers can be attributed to the trailblazing work done by MacLennan and the other members of his generation. For example, Margaret Laurence included this tribute in a letter she wrote to MacLennan:

> I feel very deeply that I owe you a debt of gratitude as a novelist. It was really only through your novels, and those of Ethel Wilson, and Sinclair Ross, and very few others, that I came to an understanding of the simple fact that novels could be written *here,* out of one's own background, and that in fact this was the only true soil for me to write out of.[3]

MacLennan is often seen as primarily a political novelist, the author of near-allegorical fables about Canada's coming-of-age, in which characterization is a secondary issue. Certainly he is the most self-conscious literary nationalist of his generation, and his characters move through the corridors of power more often than the characters of any Canadian novelist except Richard Rohmer—if Rohmer can be considered a novelist. MacLennan's depiction of characters who are integral parts of a specifically Canadian social and political background make his novels permanent landmarks in the development of Canadian fiction. But MacLennan's novels are more than simply a set of variations on the theme of Canadian national identity.

Throughout his career, MacLennan has sought to affirm the best features of his Protestant heritage, while criticizing the self-mortifying outlook caused by, as he once told his father, "the asceticism which St. Paul foisted on Christianity."[4] In consequence, MacLennan's fiction has made a significant contribution to the study of the culture of guilt that is examined by so many Canadian novelists, from Ralph Connor in *The Man from Glengarry* right through to Margaret Laurence and Sinclair Ross, and more recently, Margaret Atwood, Alice Munro, and Marian Engel. MacLennan's novels depict a gradual acknowledgment of the crippling effects of Calvinist guilt and then an acceptance of the human shortcomings that cause such guilt. Slowly, MacLennan's characters have learned the lesson that Father Blazon and Liesl urge on Dunstan Ramsay in Robertson Davies's *Fifth Business* when they advise him to accept his normal human failings.

Although MacLennan has tried to present a more comprehensive picture of the workings of society than has any other writer of his generation, his accomplishments have often failed to measure up to his aims. His own fiction often lacks sensitivity to nuances of either character or language and usually is marked by an unsubtle narrative technique. With the exception of *The Watch That Ends the Night*, MacLennan has not written a novel that rises above its time and place of composition to become a purely artistic landmark, rather than a record of a stage in Canada's political and social history. Like another important figure in the Canadian tradition, Frederick Philip Grove, MacLennan is a compelling writer in spite of weaknesses that might destroy the work of an author with a less urgent message.

It seems likely that MacLennan never achieved his full potential as a novelist. He is a born storyteller who was taught at an early age to distrust the supposedly frivolous pleasure that comes from telling or listening to mere stories. Writing always with Dr. Sam's spirit looking over his shoulder, MacLennan has sought to create fiction that serves an obvious social and moral purpose. He has never felt free to let his interest in a story per se determine where his narrative should go. His greatest gifts are for portraying near-melodramatic psychological conflicts, usually arising within a family setting, and for evoking the eternally recurrent human wish to return to a simpler and more secure world, essentially a continuation of childhood. In short, MacLennan has a romantic temperament. However, he has spent much of his career unhappily trying to meet the expectations of an ironic and realistic age or battling against the standards of such an age.

The most influential discussion of MacLennan's fiction is undoubtedly George Woodcock's pioneering essay, "A Nation's Odyssey: The Novels of Hugh MacLennan."[5] Woodcock argued, as he later explained, that the "great unifying myth of MacLennan's novels was the *Odyssey* translated into terms of modern life."[6] Woodcock's viewpoint has gained such wide currency that not enough attention has been paid to a suggestive study by Alec Lucas, who adroitly points out the unsuitability of the *Odyssey* as a mythic paradigm for MacLennan's fiction, especially for his early novels: "Ulysses was an old man bringing hopes of restoring the old order in a disordered society. Neil Macrae and other wayfarers are young men bringing hopes of setting up a new order in a disordered society."[7]

Lucas effectively argues that the most appropriate classical parallel for MacLennan's habitual plot structures is the story of Oedipus. He lists the motifs from the Oedipus myth as recurrent elements in MacLennan's novels: "heroes with physical defects; the return of allegedly dead men; the separation from the father; the search for a father during which the son, by growing up, unconsciously destroys the father image and, like Oedipus, in trying simultaneously to find the reason for a resultant uncertainty, discovers himself." To this list of parallels might be added a childhood presided over by kindly foster-parents, and sexual attraction to a member of one's own family or to a maternal female.

Lucas explains the parallels between MacLennan's fiction and the Oedipus myth by alluding to MacLennan's great admiration for Sophocles' Theban plays. However, there is a more fundamental reason why MacLennan's novels should be viewed as versions of the Oedipus legend rather than as retellings of the *Odyssey*. The emotional issues that are central to MacLennan's fiction are precisely the issues that are present in the Oedipus myth. The story of Oedipus serves in psychoanalytic thought as a primary model for discussing masculine psychology. The myth provides the name for an important phase of childhood development, in which attachment to the mother is still strong and the father is seen as a rival for the mother's affections and attention. The resulting hostility toward the father is dramatically acted out in the myth when Oedipus kills his own father. In MacLennan's novels, the sons do not literally slay their fathers, but they do frequently feel strong antagonism toward a father figure. And their attraction to a maternal female is often part and parcel of their conflict with this father figure. In MacLennan's novels, as in the story of Oedipus, the presentation of women is strikingly ambivalent, combining sexual attractiveness with the power to create a ruinous conflict between father and son. The Oedipus myth presents man as a homeless wanderer in a hostile universe and explains this condition as the result of a tragic fall from innocence into guilty knowledge. This motif can frequently be found in MacLennan's novels.

The Oedipus story culminates in the revelation of a sexual relationship between a mother and a son. It is not only his violation of the incest taboo that shocks Oedipus but also his sudden recognition of sexuality in the mother. With this knowledge comes an unavoidable awareness that the father's relationship to the mother was also sexual. Therefore, a significant though seldom noticed aspect of the Oedipus myth is the sudden disclosure of parental sexuality, a discovery that comes upon Oedipus with all the shocking impact of an actual Freudian primal scene. Oedipus has, albeit unknowingly, clung to a sheltered position beside his mother; from a psychoanalytic viewpoint, he should have recognized that true maturity does not consist of taking the father's place but of making one's own way in the world.

The Oedipus myth presents an image of mankind trying to emerge from the shadow of the parents and live an independent life. This is also the task that faces the younger generation in MacLennan's fiction. Taken in their entirety, MacLennan's novels constitute a searching examination of the way Oedipal conflicts may influence the lives of individuals. However, in the three novels from the later stages of MacLennan's career, the conflict between generations has a different outcome than it has in his earlier books. His first three published novels, as well as his two unpublished works, are written from the younger generation's viewpoint and show youth in rebellion against restrictive parental figures. However, the generational conflict is evaded rather than fully resolved in the denouements of these stories. With *Each Man's Son,* MacLennan's fiction enters a new phase. This novel shows a son grown into middle age, who at last recognizes the futility of his lifelong inner quarrel with the ghost of his father. This realization frees Dr. Ainslie to start a family of his own. In MacLennan's next two novels, the protagonists value their paternal roles very highly, yet are not overly possessive of their children. George Stewart and Alan Ainslie each launch a daughter into marriage; therefore, for Sally Martell and Chantal Ainslie the family is not imprisoning but supportive. And in *Voices in Time,* John Wellfleet adopts a paternal attitude toward the entire human race.

From whatever angle it is examined, MacLennan's career as a novelist follows a path from a youthful rebellion against the values of the parental generation to an eventual acceptance of those same values. For example, MacLennan started his literary career by emulating Joyce and Hemingway; thereby he joined a widespread rejection by younger writers of Victorian and Edwardian literary modes. Yet, later in his career, MacLennan has drawn upon the example of older novelists of the British and European traditions. His conception of the novel as a social document owes more to the examples of Galsworthy and Tolstoy than to the precedents set by Joyce or Hemingway or any other modernist writer. Philosophically, MacLennan's outlook has also undergone a shift from rebellion to acquiescence. After an early flirtation with the materialistic determinism of Marxian and Freudian thought, he has returned to the religion of his forefathers. Although in *Return of the Sphinx* Alan Ainslie announces the death of what he calls the Victorian outlook, this outlook is actually the viewpoint that George Stewart triumphantly learns to accept in *The Watch That Ends the Night*. *Voices in Time* portrays the self-destruction of the modern technological world and the re-emergence of a society based on the traditional values MacLennan has come to see as essential to the continued survival of human society on earth.

Read in chronological order, MacLennan's novels record a slow and difficult growth to maturity. Above all, there is an increasingly explicit recognition of the complexity of most emotional questions. In the early novels, stern and kindly traits are assigned to separate characters, but in the later novels the same character can be both oppressive and loving. The increasingly complex portrayal of human feelings reflects important developments within MacLennan himself. Before he could make his peace with a world toward which he had long held a grudge, MacLennan needed to accept himself. He needed to acknowledge the complexity of human nature—his own included. MacLennan's acceptance of humanity's less admirable aspects is evident throughout his later fiction, and his acceptance of himself is signaled above all by his creation of the fallible and long-suffering George Stewart. *The Watch That Ends the Night* marks a watershed in MacLennan's development, announcing his attainment of a truly mature outlook. This novel represents MacLennan's most harmonious synthesis of all aspects of his artistry and thought.

MacLennan's quarrel with the parental generation, despite being based on an extension of the Oedipal conflicts, has not had a destructive outcome. He has, albeit with difficulty, reconciled the demanding father-within-himself with the part of him that has remained a rebellious son. Indeed, the conservative and traditional values of the parental generation came to seem a supportive framework to which MacLennan, as the lonely representative of the younger generation, turned for support when his sense of isolation in a meaningless universe became too great to be endured. In emotional, artistic, religious, and philosophical terms, MacLennan has learned to live in his father's house.

Essayist

In addition to the fiction for which he is best known, MacLennan has produced a considerable body of nonfiction. His essays can be divided into two groups: first, what he terms think pieces, in which he treats questions of public importance in a solemn, analytical manner, and second, the familiar essays, in which he adopts a more personal tone and treats a greater variety of subjects, both trivial and weighty. Most of the think pieces are not enduring works, but they do give a good picture of MacLennan's intellectual preoccupations. The most important themes of these pieces are the nature of Canada, the nature of modern society, and the place of literature in the modern world. The common denominator in MacLennan's treatment of these topics is his conservatism.

MacLennan is a convinced antimodernist, in the sense that he sees only harm arising from the uncontrolled growth of technology and of the bureaucracy needed to run a technological society. He also objects to the major trends he sees in modern literature. Instead, he would retain both traditional social beliefs and traditional forms of fiction. He sees Canada as a place where the progressive ideology has not attained the dominance it has achieved in the United States. Indeed, MacLennan has often argued that Canada's conservatism could serve as a salutary lesson to the modern world. The lesson would be twofold: Canada has not wholly succumbed to the blandishments of consumerism, and Canada can provide an example of different ethnic groups living in relative harmony.

MacLennan will not be remembered as a powerful or original thinker. His analysis of Canada's national identity is too narrow to win general assent, and his conception of Canada's mission has an evangelical fervor that is difficult for others to share. His literary criticism is based on a limited and prescriptive conception of the novel, which undervalues much of the best fiction of our century. MacLennan's critical writings and many of his essays on Canada are important, not for their ideas per se, but for the polemical program they enunciate, a program that underlies MacLennan's own novels.

MacLennan's best nonfiction is found not in his think pieces but in those essays that are more intimate and confessional. Indeed, in the fifties MacLennan became one of Canada's most skilled practitioners of that difficult form, the familiar essay. In his unbuttoned moments, particularly in a number of the essays written for the *Montrealer,* MacLennan projects an appealing, entertaining personality. He seems a cultivated and genteel raconteur, a civilized man frequently ill at ease in a barbarous time. His nostalgic reminiscences of Cape Breton and of Oxford are often superbly done. In his best familiar essays, MacLennan is an amiable and contemplative conversationalist, gracefully embellishing whatever topic comes to hand, bringing wit and erudition to bear on subjects both frivolous and serious. Here he frequently sounds the elegiac note that occurs so often in his fiction. As he laments the passing of a more leisurely and mannered age, the force of his eloquence often wins the reader to share, however briefly, a feeling of loss at the fading of customs and values that once exerted a stabilizing effect on society.

Writer *Engagé*

Although MacLennan has not advocated a specific political or social doctrine, he has always filled the role he describes as "writer *engagé*." "My own notion of the *engagé*," he explains, "has nothing to do with politics in the ordinary sense. I think of a man whose temperament compels him to involve himself in his time, to live with his antennae naked to the stimuli of his time because he belongs to it."[8] MacLennan has never seen himself as a Joycean detached observer, paring his fingernails while the world goes to ruin. Filled with both dismay and compassion, he has recorded the psychic stresses that two World Wars, a Depression, and the threat of nuclear holocaust have imposed on anyone who cannot limit his awareness to an area of narrowly personal concerns. His writings show how one individual, working against the grain of his society, has maintained a coherent vision of the worth of the individual in a world dominated by vast bureaucratic organizations and the mass-men who run them.

In all his writing, MacLennan has expressed the conservative principles that are characteristic of much that is best in the Canadian intellectual tradition. MacLennan's books are cut from the same Tory cloth as the history of Donald Creighton and the philosophy of George Grant. Perhaps MacLennan is best understood as continuing the battle between humanists and modernists that was waged in North American intellectual circles during the twenties and thirties. At Princeton, MacLennan was acquainted with advocates of the modernist position; however, his classical training and his own temperament impelled him in another direction.

He has consistently maintained the humanist position that man cannot be understood in wholly rational or wholly materialist terms. He has echoed the insistence of the new humanists that in the twentieth century the "great foe is this worldliness, obsession with physical things that bind us to this animal order."[9] MacLennan understands the humanist's prime commandment to "know thyself" as a call to morality, not as a license to sensual indulgence in the name of self-development. He holds that each human personality must assume "the responsibility of bettering itself" morally; and he argues, as did the new humanists, that "true pleasure depends upon intelligent self-discipline."[10] MacLennan's viewpoint is less dogmatically expressed than are the ideas of Irving Babbitt, but he agrees with Babbitt in using ethical and intellectual criteria to make esthetic judgments. Like Paul Elmer More, MacLennan abhors modern literature that sees the world as a "Protean flux of meaningless change."[11]

Nonetheless, although MacLennan has read many of the same texts as these two high priests of new humanism, he preaches a low-church version of their faith. What matters to MacLennan is not that the "correct" opinions be adhered to but that questions about fundamental issues should not be lost from sight in society's eagerness to find "practical" solutions to immediate material "problems." In a discussion of the continuing value of the classical tradition in the modern world, MacLennan writes: "But what is truth? What is the purpose of life? What is God's will?—what matters here is not that these questions can never be adequately answered. What matters is that they must be *asked* if a society is to survive." In the same discussion, he affirms that education—and he really means life itself—is "at its best a pilgrim's progress to the heavenly city."[12] All his life, MacLennan has aspired to make such a pilgrimage.

Although MacLennan's ideas have been influenced by those two potent shapers of the modern concepts of the mind and of society, Freud and Marx, he has in the end rejected the materialistic assumptions of these thinkers and insisted on holding to his own idiosyncratic version of a spiritual or religious outlook. MacLennan rebelled against the rule of fear that he found at the heart of his father's Presbyterianism, but he did not reject a religious view of mankind. He wanted to replace the Calvinist God with a kinder deity and to reconcile the religious attitude with the findings of modern science. He took great satisfaction in the assertion made by one of his intellectual heroes, the neurosurgeon Wilder Penfield, that despite science's best efforts, the real nature of the mind remains a mystery. In language reminiscent of *The Watch That Ends the Night,* he argues: "The mysterious mind he [Penfield] described is at least immanent in the infinitely larger mystery our ancestors called 'God' and which the scientists—to avoid the superstitions of religious bureaucracies—call 'Nature.'"[13] An insistence that mankind has a spiritual as well as a material dimension is found in several of MacLennan's essays and is an important theme in most of his novels, which Alex Lucas has very appropriately described as "parables centred on religious humanism."[14]

It would be wrong to describe MacLennan's critique of the modernist position without mentioning his debt to the language and logic of Albert Jay Nock's amusingly eccentric autobiography, *Memoirs of a Superfluous Man.* For nearly forty years, MacLennan's speeches and articles have been peppered with allusions, both acknowledged and unacknowledged, to Nock's ideas.[15] At first sight, the affinity between MacLennan, the conservative, and Nock, the anarchist, is a surprising one. It is based on the fact that both men feel themselves outsiders in modern society; both feel "superfluous." Moreover, both men intensely dislike the materialism that prevails in modern North America. MacLennan insists that no one can deny Nock's thesis "that in this age the chief end of man is to produce, distribute, and consume more material goods—to which I myself later added 'and to move expensive objects from place to place at constantly increasing rates of speed.'"[16] But with their loathing for the consumer society and the progressive outlook, the similarities between the two men end.

Nock is a gadfly and ironist, who glories in his exclusion from mass society; MacLennan laments his isolation. Nock is delighted with his own outrageous pronouncements and makes railery an end in itself. MacLennan's commitment to the values embedded in the classical tradition prevents him from sharing Nock's irresponsible delight at exposing human folly. Nock retreats into the isolation of his own intellect, which he feels is vastly superior to the mind of the average mass-man. MacLennan sees every individual, whether superior or ordinary, as an infinitesimal part of some larger entity, whose nature and purpose can only be dimly apprehended by intuition rather than by reason. Ultimately, MacLennan is not concerned with material conditions but with salvation—both individual salvation and the salvation of society.

MacLennan continues to occupy what George Woodcock once termed "a position of uneasy eminence in Canadian letters."[17] In the long run, MacLennan will not be known as Canada's best novelist, but he is, as Edmund Wilson remarked, the Canadian author who has best filled the role of Balzacian "secretary to society."[18] His conservatism, his nationalism, and his affirmation of the value of the individual are distillations of attitudes held by many Canadians. To belittle MacLennan's work because his ideas are out of style, or because his fiction is not avant-garde and experimental in form is to show a limited understanding of the range of both human and literary possibilities. The subjects MacLennan treats and the attitudes he expresses are intensely meaningful to many people who feel themselves out of sympathy with the raging materialism that dominates modern culture. To speak for this group of readers is no inconsiderable accomplishment. MacLennan remains the most representative man of letters of his generation, and one of the most imposing literary figures Canada has yet produced.

Notes and References

Most of the unpublished materials cited below are located in the Hugh MacLennan Papers, Department of Rare Books and Special Collections, McGill University Libraries, or in the Hugh MacLennan Papers, Special Collections Division, University of Calgary Library. The letters from MacLennan to George Barrett are in the Archives, McCord Museum, Montreal.

Preface

1. MacLennan to Cowan, 11 October 1968, Calgary, file 3.11.16.
2. A film version of *Two Solitudes,* made by another producer, was released in 1978.
3. Fyodor Dostoyevsky, *Notes from Underground/The Double,* trans. Jessie Coulson (Harmondsworth, England: Penguin, 1972), p. 45.

Chapter One

1. Hugh MacLennan, Introduction, in *The Inner Ocean: Paintings and Drawings by Ron Bolt* (Toronto: Merritt Publishing Co. 1979), p. 11.
2. "The Anatomy of Humour," in *Thirty and Three,* ed. Dorothy Duncan (Toronto, 1954), p. 237.
3. Elspeth Cameron, *Hugh MacLennan: A Writer's Life* (Toronto, 1981), p. 282 and passim.
4. "The Scottish Touch: Cape Breton," in *The Other Side of Hugh MacLennan,* ed. Elspeth Cameron (Toronto, 1978), p. 215.
5. "Scotchman's Return," in *Scotchman's Return and Other Essays* (Toronto, 1960), pp. 1–2.
6. "The Scottish Touch: Cape Breton," in *The Other Side,* p. 216.
7. Cameron, *A Writer's Life,* p. 4.
8. The story of his father's departure and subsequent return is told by MacLennan in "An Orange from Portugal," in *Cross-Country* (1949; reprint ed., Edmonton: Hurtig, 1972), pp. 26–29.
9. Cameron, *A Writer's Life,* pp. 10–11.
10. "Portrait of a City," in *Cross-Country,* p. 102. MacLennan has exercised some artistic freedom here. Cameron reports that he was actually at home at the moment the explosion occurred; see *A Writer's Life,* p. 13.
11. "Concussion," *Lower Canada College Magazine,* June 1938, p. 28.

12. "On Living in a Cold Country," in *The Other Side,* pp. 208–9.
13. "New York, New York," in *Scotchman's Return,* p. 136.
14. *Return of the Sphinx* (Toronto, 1967), p. 143.
15. Many of MacLennan's letters from Oxford are housed in the McGill collection; the story about hearing Galsworthy is told in "The Future of the Novel," a speech given to the Vermont League of Writers, 13 July 1961. A copy is located at McGill, file 1.1.7.
16. "And Seeing the Multitudes," *Lower Canada College Magazine,* February 1937, pp. 9–14.
17. "A Modest Proposal," in *Thirty and Three,* pp. 193–94.
18. Hugh MacLennan to Samuel MacLennan, 28 December 1931, McGill, file 1.2.3.
19. Hugh MacLennan to Frances MacLennan, 22 January 1932, McGill, file 1.2.10. Cameron prints some examples of MacLennan's poetry: see *A Writer's Life,* pp. 52, 53, 57.
20. But Cameron reports that the other man's grades were better than MacLennan's; see *A Writer's Life,* pp. 43, 62, 72.
21. The entire incident is described in "On Discovering Who We Are," in *Cross-Country,* pp. 39–41.
22. The last two quotations are from "The Future of the Novel as an Art Form," in *Scotchman's Return,* p. 143.
23. "The Writer *Engagé,*" in *The Other Side,* p. 278.
24. "Husband and Wife," in *Thirty and Three,* p. 21.
25. "The Story of a Novel," in *Masks of Fiction,* ed. A. J. M. Smith (Toronto: McClelland & Stewart, 1961), p. 36.
26. The letters are located at Calgary, file 3.1.
27. Cameron, *A Writer's Life,* p. 121.
28. Sigmund Freud, "Family Romances," in *The Standard Edition of the Complete Psychological Works of Sigmund Freud,* ed. James Strachey (London: Hogarth Press, 1959), 9:237–41. The quotations used in the text are from pp. 237, 240–41.

Chapter Two

1. The last two quotations are from *Two Solitudes* (Toronto, 1945), pp. 306, 307.
2. The manuscript is located at McGill, files 3.1.1–2; the title comes from Shakespeare, Sonnet 106.
3. *Oxyrhynchus: An Economic and Social Study* (1935; reprint ed., Amsterdam: Hakkert, 1968); hereafter page references cited in the text.
4. The last two quotations are from "Oxyrhynchus," *Dalhousie Review* 16 (October 1936):315, 316.
5. "Roman History and To-Day," *Dalhousie Review* 15 (April 1935):67–78. The quotations in the text are from pp. 67, 69, 70, 71, 78.

Notes and References 131

6. The manuscript is located at McGill, files 3.1.3–9. There are two drafts: files 3.1.3–6 contain a longer and apparently earlier version; files 3.1.7–9 contain a revised version. The title comes from Ecclesiastes 3:22.
7. The last three quotations are from MacLennan to Barrett, 5 March 1935, McCord.
8. This character is called Anne Lovelace in the earlier draft of the novel. Cameron uses the name Anne Lovelace in *A Writer's Life,* pp. 109–10.

Chapter Three

1. Foreword, in *Barometer Rising* (Toronto, 1941); hereafter page references cited in the text.
2. *Two Solitudes* (Toronto, 1945), p. 329; hereafter page references cited in the text.
3. MacLennan to Barrett, 16 November 1942, McCord.
4. Cameron, *A Writer's Life,* p. 139.
5. MacLennan to Barrett, 20 October 1941, McCord.
6. The last two quotations are from MacLennan to Barrett, 16 November 1942, McCord.
7. Naim Kattan, "Montreal and French-Canadian Culture," *Tamarack Review,* no. 40 (Summer 1966), p. 53.
8. Anonymous letter to MacLennan, McGill, file 1.2.11.
9. MacLennan, application for a Guggenheim Fellowship, 26 October 1942, McGill, file 1.1.1.

Chapter Four

1. "Canada between Covers," *Saturday Review of Literature,* 7 September 1946, p. 30. The quotations in the next paragraph are also from p. 30.
2. *The Precipice* (Toronto, 1948), p. 105; hereafter page references cited in the text.
3. Quoted by Hugo MacPherson, "The Novels of Hugh MacLennan," in *Hugh MacLennan,* ed. Paul Goetsch (Toronto, 1973), p. 28.
4. *Each Man's Son* (Toronto, 1951), p. 85; hereafter page references cited in the text.
5. *Two Solitudes,* p. 259.
6. *Two Solitudes,* p. 328.
7. The last three quotations are from "Cape Breton: The Legendary Isle," *Saturday Night,* 3 July 1951, pp. 12–13.
8. MacLennan to Gray, 12 August 1950, McGill, file 1.1.3.
9. "My Surgeon Father," *Bulletin of the American College of Surgeons* 44 (July-August 1959):214.
10. "A Layman Looks at Medical Men," *Canadian Doctor* 18 (December 1952):35.

11. Alan Twigg, "Patricius," in *For Openers* (Madeira Park, B.C., 1981), p. 95.
12. "A Layman Looks at Medical Men," p. 95.
13. "The Scottish Touch: Cape Breton," in *The Other Side,* p. 216.
14. The three quotations from Tallman's article are from "Wolf in the Snow," in *Contexts of Canadian Criticism,* ed. Eli Mandel (Chicago, 1971), pp. 243–45.

Chapter Five

1. This quotation and the quotations in the preceding paragraph are from "Victory," in *The Other Side,* pp. 179, 182, 183.
2. *The Watch That Ends the Night* (Toronto, 1959), p. 373; hereafter page references cited in the text. The title, suggested by the American publisher, comes from the hymn "O, God, Our Help in Ages Past"; see Cameron, *A Writer's Life,* p. 295.
3. The last two quotations are from "A Word Aside," in *Thirty and Three,* pp. vii, viii.
4. "Prologue: The Writer and His Audience," in *The Other Side,* pp. 2,3.
5. "Homage to Hemingway," in *Thirty and Three,* pp. 85–96. The quotations used in the text are from pp. 93–95.
6. "Changing Values in Fiction," *Canadian Author and Bookman* 25 (August 1949):10–18. The quotations in the text are from pp. 15–17.
7. "Reflections on Two Decades," in *The Other Side,* p. 247.
8. Cameron, *A Writer's Life,* p. 285.
9. MacLennan speaks of Dr. Rabinovitch as one of the models for Jerome Martell in a letter to the *Montreal Star,* 27 September 1965.
10. Dorothy Farmiloe, "Hugh MacLennan and the Canadian Myth," in *Hugh MacLennan,* ed. Goetsch, pp. 145–54.
11. "Reflections on Two Decades," in *The Other Side,* p. 252.
12. "Are We a Godless People?" *Maclean's,* 15 March 1949, pp. 7, 71–77.
13. The quotations in this paragraph and in the preceding paragraph are from *Cross-Country,* pp. 140, 153, 154.

Chapter Six

1. *The Watch That Ends the Night,* p. 4.
2. *The Present World as Seen in Its Literature* (Fredericton: University of New Brunswick, 1952), p. 12.
3. The last two quotations are from "It Pays to Pamper Our Children," *Maclean's,* 21 July 1956, p. 48.
4. Gordon Rattray Taylor, *Sex in History* (London: Thames & Hudson, 1953).
5. "Reflections on *Sex in History,*" *Montreal Star,* 8 September 1962, Entertainments, p. 5.

6. MacLennan to Wilson, 20 February 1968, Calgary, file 3.4.53.
7. "Reflections on Two Decades," in *The Other Side,* pp. 247–59. The quotations in the text are from pp. 247, 251, 255.
8. The last two quotations are from "Off to Write a Novel, MacLennan Says Goodbye," *Montreal Star,* 5 October 1963, Entertainments, p. 4.
9. MacLennan to Wilson, 15 June 1968, Calgary, file 3.4.53.
10. Peter Buitenhuis, *Hugh MacLennan* (Toronto, 1969), p. 69.
11. *Return of the Sphinx* (Toronto, 1967); hereafter page references cited in the text. The title and the framework for the novel's plot are derived from Sophocles' *Oedipus at Colonus:* Cameron, *A Writer's Life,* pp. 319–21, 327–28.
12. "Reflections on Two Decades," in *The Other Side,* p. 256.
13. Ibid., pp. 257–58.
14. "The Physiology and Psychology of Cussing," *Montreal Star,* 13 July 1963, Entertainments, p. 4.
15. MacLennan to Cockburn, 1 May 1970, Calgary, file 3.4.14.
16. Alan Twigg, "Patricius," in *For Openers,* p. 85.
17. *Rivers of Canada* (Toronto, 1974), p. 7; hereafter page references cited in the text.
18. *Voices in Time* (Toronto, 1980), pp. 42–43; hereafter page references cited in the text.
19. Cameron, *A Writer's Life,* pp. 357–58.
20. Introduction, in *The Time-Gatherers,* ed. Gertrude Katz (Montreal: Harvest House, 1970), p. 4.

Chapter Seven

1. George Woodcock, "Surrogate Fathers and Orphan Sons," *Journal of Canadian Studies* 14 (Winter 1979–80):21.
2. MacLennan to Goetsch, 6 October 1959. Quoted in Goetsch, ed., *Hugh MacLennan,* p. 3.
3. Laurence to MacLennan, 16 February 1970, Calgary, file 3.3.44.
4. Hugh MacLennan to Samuel MacLennan, 28 December 1931, McGill, file 1.2.3.
5. George Woodcock, "A Nation's Odyssey: The novels of Hugh MacLennan," *Canadian Literature,* no. 10 (Autumn 1961), pp. 7–18.
6. George Woodcock, *Hugh MacLennan* (Toronto, 1969), p. 52.
7. This quotation and the quotation in the next paragraph are from Alec Lucas, *Hugh MacLennan* (Toronto, 1970), pp. 47, 47–48.
8. "The Writer *Engagé,*" in *The Other Side,* p. 270.
9. Norman Foerster, Preface, in *Humanism and America,* ed. Norman Foerster (1930; reprint ed., Port Washington, N.Y.: Kennikat Press, 1967), p. x.
10. "Humanism Today," a paper presented to the School-University Conference at McGill University, 5 November 1966. A copy is located at Calgary, file 1.2.25.

11. Quoted in David Hoeveler, Jr., *The New Humanism: A Critique of Modern America, 1900–1940* (Charlottesville: University Press of Virginia, 1977), p. 102. However, MacLennan denies that the new humanists exerted any direct influence on his thinking: MacLennan to the author, 21 September 1981.
12. "The Classical Tradition and Education," in *Scotchman's Return*, p. 75.
13. "The Writer *Engagé*," in *The Other Side*, p. 286.
14. Lucas, *Hugh MacLennan*, p. 57.
15. For MacLennan's most extensive comments on Nock, see: "Speaking of Books," *New York Times Book Review*, 30 September 1962, p. 2; Foreword, in Albert Jay Nock, *Memoirs of a Superfluous Man* (Chicago: Regnery, 1964).
16. Foreword, *Memoirs*, p. vi. MacLennan has used this idea, with slightly different phrasing, on several occasions. In the manuscript of "A Man Should Rejoice," he makes David Culver say: "Even if all our civilization amounts to is inventing ways of getting quicker each year from New York to Chicago and shifting big objects from one place to another, I guess it's what we were born to" (McGill, file 3.1.7). In *Two Solitudes*, Paul Tallard says of Kathleen's second husband, an American, that life "to him was fun and business, and business consisted in making money and moving large objects from one place to another" (p. 250).
17. Woodcock, *Hugh MacLennan*, p. 1.
18. Edmund Wilson, *O Canada* (New York, 1965), p. 68.

Selected Bibliography

PRIMARY SOURCES

1. Novels
Barometer Rising. New York: Duell, Sloan & Pearce, 1941; Toronto: Collins, 1941; London: Harrap, 1942.
Two Solitudes. New York: Duell, Sloan & Pearce, 1945; Toronto: Collins, 1945; London: Cresset, 1946.
The Precipice. New York: Duell, Sloan & Pearce, 1948; Toronto: Collins, 1948; London: Cresset, 1949.
Each Man's Son. Boston: Little, Brown & Co., 1951; Toronto: Macmillan, 1951; London: Heinemann. 1952.
The Watch That Ends the Night. New York: Scribner's, 1959; Toronto: Macmillan, 1959; London: Heinemann, 1959.
Return of the Sphinx. New York: Scribner's, 1967; Toronto: Macmillan, 1967.
Voices in Time. Toronto: Macmillan, 1980.

2. NonFiction
Oxyrhynchus: An Economic and Social Study. Princeton: Princeton University Press, 1935.
Cross-Country. Toronto: Collins, 1949.
Thirty and Three. Edited by Dorothy Duncan. Toronto: Macmillan, 1954; London: Macmillan & Co., 1955.
Scotchman's Return and Other Essays. Toronto: Macmillan, 1960; New York: Scribner's, 1960; London: Macmillan & Co., 1960.
McGill: The Story of a University. Edited by Hugh MacLennan. London: Allen & Unwin, 1960.
Seven Rivers of Canada. Toronto: Macmillan, 1961; New York: Scribner's, 1961.
The Colour of Canada. The Canadian Illustrated Library. Toronto: McClelland & Stewart, 1967; Boston: Little, Brown & Co., 1967.
Rivers of Canada. Illustrated with photographs by John de Visser. Toronto: Macmillan, 1974.
The Other Side of Hugh MacLennan: Selected Essays Old and New. Edited by Elspeth Cameron. Toronto: Macmillan, 1978.

3. Unpublished Materials
The principal collections of unpublished manuscripts and letters are the Hugh MacLennan Papers, Department of Rare Books and Special Collections, McGill University Libraries, Montreal, and the Hugh MacLennan Papers, Special Collections Division, University of Calgary Library, Calgary. MacLennan's letters to George Barrett are in the Archives, McCord Museum, Montreal. Some letters and manuscripts are in the Thomas Fisher Rare Book Library, University of Toronto, Toronto. MacLennan's correspondence with Macmillan of Canada is in the Macmillan Archive, McMaster University, Hamilton.

SECONDARY SOURCES

1. Bibliography
Cameron, Elspeth. "Hugh MacLennan: An Annotated Bibliography." In *The Annotated Bibliography of Canada's Major Authors*. Edited by Robert Lecker and Jack David. Vol. I. Downsview, Ont.: ECW Press, 1979, pp. 103–52. Lists MacLennan's books, pamphlets, and articles. Gives useful annotated lists of secondary materials.

2. Books and Collections of Articles
Buitenhuis, Peter. *Hugh MacLennan*. Canadian Writers and Their Works. Toronto: Coles, 1969. An introductory survey of the novels. Gives a good assessment of MacLennan's historical place in the development of Canadian fiction.
Cameron, Elspeth. *Hugh MacLennan: A Writer's Life*. Toronto: University of Toronto Press, 1981. A full-scale biography. Sees MacLennan's father as the primary influence on his early life. Gives detailed accounts of the writing, publication, and intial reception of MacLennan's novels.
Cockburn, Robert H. *The Novels of Hugh MacLennan*. Montreal: Harvest House, 1969. Criticizes MacLennan severely for his didacticism and his repetitive characterizations.
Goetsch, Paul, ed. *Hugh MacLennan*. Critical Views on Canadian Writers. Toronto: McGraw-Hill Ryerson, 1973. Reprints several articles and selected reviews of all the novels before *Voices in Time*. Includes the articles by McPherson, New, Hirano, and Farmiloe listed below.
Goetsch, Paul. *Das Romanwerk Hugh MacLennans: Eine Studie zum literarischen Nationalismus in Kanada*. Hamburg: Cram, de Gruyter, 1961. Not available in English translation, but see article by Goetsch listed below.
Heintzmann, Ralph, ed. *Journal of Canadian Studies* 14 (Winter 1979–80). A special issue on MacLennan. Includes a discussion of the critical response to MacLennan's work and a chronological listing of major events in MacLen-

nan's life, both by Elspeth Cameron. Contains the articles by Bonnycastle, Hoy, and Zichy listed below.

Lucas, Alec. *Hugh MacLennan.* Canadian Writers, no. 8. Toronto: McClelland & Stewart, 1970. An introductory survey of the themes and techniques of MacLennan's fiction. Argues that MacLennan has adapted the popular romance to express his serious social and political concerns.

Morley, Patricia. *The Immoral Moralists: Hugh MacLennan and Leonard Cohen.* Toronto: Clarke, Irwin, 1972. Questions MacLennan's portrayal of puritanism as a wholly negative force. Uses the novels of MacLennan and Cohen to illustrate changing attitudes and values in modern Canadian society.

Woodcock, George. *Hugh MacLennan.* Studies in Canadian Literature. Toronto: Copp Clark, 1969. Expands the argument of Woodcock's essay "A Nation's Odyssey," listed below. The early chapters provide a useful summary of the main ideas expressed in MacLennan's essays.

3. Articles, Interviews, and Parts of Books

Bonnycastle, Stephen. "The Power of *The Watch That Ends the Night.*" *Journal of Canadian Studies* 14 (Winter 1979–80):76–89. An ambitious attempt to apply structuralist methods to MacLennan's novel. The essay approvingly points out resemblances between MacLennan's philosophy and the outlooks of Wordsworth, Proust, and Spinoza. In practice, however, the critical procedure is less innovative than Bonnycastle claims.

Cameron, Donald. "The Tennis Racket Is an Antelope Bone." *Journal of Canadian Fiction* 1 (Winter 1972):40–47. Reprinted in *Conversations with Canadian Novelists: Part One.* Toronto: Macmillan, 1973, pp. 129–48. MacLennan's comments in this interview and in the interview with Alan Twigg listed below are particularly relevant to his last two novels.

Farmiloe, Dorothy. "Hugh MacLennan and the Canadian Myth." *Mosaic* 2 (Spring 1969):1–9. Reprinted in Goetsch, ed., *Hugh MacLennan,* pp. 145–54. Argues that in Jerome's escape down the river "MacLennan has consciously embodied in narrative form" the "myth" of the voyageur, which he sees as central to Canadian history.

Goetsch, Paul. "Too Long to the Courtly Muses: Hugh MacLennan as a Contemporary Writer." *Canadian Literature,* no. 10 (Autumn 1961), pp. 10–31. A survey of MacLennan's novels to 1959. Goetsch sees *The Watch That Ends the Night* as MacLennan's most successful book. He praises the portrayal of George Stewart and offers a Jungian reading of the novel. He concludes by defining MacLennan's place in the North American tradition in fiction.

Hirano, Keiichi. "Jerome Martell and Norman Bethune." In *Hugh MacLennan,* ed. Goetsch, pp. 123–38. Sees Jerome Martell as based on Dr. Norman Bethune, but contends that MacLennan has softened those aspects of Bethune's thinking that might disturb the reading public.

Hoy, Helen. "'The Gates Closed on Us Then': The Paradise-Lost Motif in Hugh MacLennan's Fiction." *Journal of Canadian Studies* 14 (Winter 1979–80):29–45. Contends that an underlying pattern in all of MacLennan's fiction is the loss of a paradisal world and the subsequent "search in a fallen world for a new paradise."

Hyman, Leslie Robert. "Hugh MacLennan: His Art, His Society and His Critics." *Queen's Quarterly* 32 (Winter 1975):515–28. Argues that MacLennan's novels have been overpraised because critics have wished to believe in the vision of Canada that the novels express.

Jones, D. G. *Butterfly on Rock: A Study of Themes and Images in Canadian Literature.* Toronto: University of Toronto Press, 1970, pp. 62–65, 157–62, and passim. Discusses *Each Man's Son* as a study of the fearful, life-denying dualism Jones sees throughout Western culture; discusses *The Watch That Ends the Night* as a novel in which this dualism is overcome.

McPherson, Hugo. Introduction. In *Barometer Rising*. Toronto: McClelland & Stewart, 1958, pp. ix–xv. An excellent discussion of the structure and symbolism of the novel.

———. "The Novels of Hugh MacLennan." *Queen's Quarterly* 60 (Summer 1953):186–98. Reprinted in *Hugh MacLennan,* ed. Goetsch, pp. 23–33. Argues that MacLennan succeeds when he uses simplified characterizations to reinforce the near-allegorical plots of *Barometer Rising* and *Two Solitudes,* but fails when he attempts more complex psychological portraits.

Mathews, Robin. "Hugh MacLennan: The Nationalist Dilemma." In *Canadian Literature: Surrender or Revolution.* Toronto: Steel Rail, 1978, pp. 75–90. A leftist critique of MacLennan's treatment of social and political issues. Analyzes *Barometer Rising* as a study of psychological deracination.

New, W. H. "The Storm and After: MacLennan's *Barometer Rising.*" In *Articulating West: Essays on Purpose and Form in Modern Canadian Literature.* Toronto: New Press, 1972, pp. 95–107. Reprinted in *Hugh MacLennan,* ed. Goetsch, pp. 75–87. A good analysis of the recurrent images that are used in the novel to reveal character and to clarify the themes.

Stevenson, Warren. "A Neglected Theme in *Two Solitudes.*" *Canadian Literature,* no. 75 (Winter 1977), pp. 53–60. Discusses the theme of individual self-awareness in the novel. Captain Yardley, Paul Tallard, and Heather Methuen learn to face the "ultimate solitude" of existence; Athanase Tallard, Marius Tallard, Huntly McQueen, and Janet Methuen fail to do this.

Sutherland, Ronald. *Second Image: Comparative Studies in Quebec/Canadian Literature.* Toronto: New Press, 1971, pp. 123–26 and passim. Says MacLennan is one of the few writers who portray the bicultural "mainstream" of Canadian society.

———. "Hugh MacLennan." *Canadian Literature,* no. 68–69 (Spring-Summer 1976), pp. 40–48. This interview contains informative comments on MacLennan's background and on his literary career.

Tallman, Warren. "Wolf in the Snow." *Canadian Literature*, no. 5 (Summer 1960), pp. 7–20; and *Canadian Literature*, no. 6 (Autumn 1960), pp. 41–48. Reprinted in Eli Mandel, ed. *Contexts of Canadian Criticism*. Chicago: University of Chicago Press, 1971, pp. 232–53. Contains a short discussion of *Each Man's Son*, which Tallman says exemplifies MacLennan's failure to acknowledge the deepest impulses that lie behind his fiction.

Twigg, Alan. "Patricius." In *For Openers:. Conversations with 24 Canadian Writers*. Madeira Park, B.C.: Harbour Publishing, 1981, pp. 83–96.

Wilson, Edmund. *O Canada: An American's Notes on Canadian Culture*. New York: Farrar, Straus & Giroux, 1965, pp. 59–80. Wilson's prestige, rather than the intrinsic merits of his analysis, have made this discussion influential.

Woodcock, George. "A Nation's Odyssey: The Novels of Hugh MacLennan." *Canadian Literature*, no. 10 (Autumn 1961), pp. 7–18. Reprinted in *Odysseus Ever Returning*. Toronto: McClelland & Stewart, 1970, pp. 12–23. Argues that the recurrent plot structures in MacLennan's fiction are derived from Homer's *Odyssey*. Says MacLennan's stress on political themes creates "an imposed pattern" that weakens his fiction.

Zichy, Francis. "'Shocked and Startled into Utter Banality': Characters and Circumstance in *The Watch That Ends the Night*." *Journal of Canadian Studies* 14 (Winter 1979–80):90–105. A Discussion of MacLennan's presentation of the novel's main characters. Zichy argues that MacLennan takes an overly indulgent view of the weaknesses found in the protagonists of all his novels.

Index

Ardrey, Robert, 107
Atwood, Margaret, 119

Babbitt, Irving, 125
Barrett, George, 26, 42
Bethune, Norman, 87
Buckler, Ernest, 1, 118
Buitenhuis, Peter, 99

Callaghan, Morley, 118
Cameron, Elspeth, 5, 13, 38, 85, 115
Cape Breton, Nova Scotia, 3–4, 37, 65–67, 124
Cary, Joyce, 81
Cockburn, Robert, 105
Cold war, 78
Connor, Ralph, 31; *The Man from Glengarry*, 119
Conrad, Joseph, 117
Creighton, Donald, 125

Dalhousie University, Halifax, 6, 8; *Dalhousie Review*, 23
Davies, Robertson, 118; *Fifth Business*, 120
Depression, 8, 10, 11, 17–18, 22, 48, 50, 63–64, 78, 83, 95, 112, 118, 125
Dos Passos, John: *U.S.A.*, 81
Duncan, Dorothy, 9, 10, 11, 13, 78, 94, 104, 105

Engel, Marian, 119
Erikson, Erik, 96

Freud, Sigmund: "Family Romances," 15–16

Galsworthy, John, 7, 42, 122
Goetsch, Paul, 119
Gray, John, 65
Grant, George, 125
Greene, Graham, 81
Grove, Frederick Philip, 118, 120; *The Master of the Mill*, 117

Halifax, Nova Scotia, 4–6, 9; explosion, 5–6, 32, 33, 34, 38, 39, 41, 42
Hemingway, Ernest, 20–21, 26, 50, 60–61, 80–81, 122
Hémon, Louis: *Maria Chapdelaine*, 43
Hitler, Adolph, 12, 17, 37, 95, 108, 110, 112, 114, 116

Joyce, James, 20–21, 50, 122, 125; *A Portrait of the Artist as a Young Man*, 29; *Ulysses*, 9

Laurence, Margaret, 1, 119
Lawrence, D. H.: *Lady Chatterley's Lover*, 94
Lower Canada College, Montreal, 9, 10, 11; *Lower Canada College Magazine*, 10
Lucas, Alec, 120–21, 126

McGill University, Montreal, 11, 79, 95

Maclean's Magazine, 92
MacLennan, Hugh, account of his life, 3–11; assessment of career, 1–2, 118–27; and Calvinism, 2, 3, 4, 12, 16, 53, 54, 55, 60–61, 62, 64, 66–68, 69, 70, 72, 73, 98, 119, 126; and determinism, 9, 17, 22, 25–26, 33, 39–40, 63, 102, 106; as literary nationalist, 1, 31–32, 42, 119; and Marxism, 9, 10, 24, 122, 126; and nature of Canada, 21, 35, 42–44, 47, 49, 50, 53, 55–60, 124; oedipal tensions in his fiction, 14–16, 40–42, 45, 46, 72–77, 86–91, 98, 99–100, 101, 105–106, 113–14, 120, 121–23; and psychoanalytic ideas, 23–24, 61–62, 96–98, 112, 122, 126; relationship with his father, 4, 6, 11–14, 22, 25, 41–42, 64, 66, 67, 70–72, 77, 87, 98, 120, 126; and technology, 17, 25, 37, 49, 51, 52; view of modern literature, 9, 20–21, 26, 60–61, 79, 80–81, 120, 124

WORKS: FICTION:
Barometer Rising, 1, 2, 6, 11, 14, 21, 31, *32–42,* 43, 44, 46, 50, 52, 55, 84
Each Man's Son, 2, 4, 11, 36, 53, 54, 56, *64–77,* 91, 98, 103
"Man Should Rejoice, A," 10, 12, 14, 26–30, 32, 36, 51, 82, 117
Precipice, The, 1, 2, 11, 29, 32, 47, 53, *54–64,* 66, 74, 84, 99, 108
Return of the Sphinx, 2, 7, 11, 54, *98–106,* 108, 109, 122
"So All Their Praises," 9, *17–22,* 30, 112, 117
Two Solitudes, 1, 2, 10, 11, 17, 29, 31, 32, *42–52,* 55, 60, 63, 74, 84

Voices in Time, 2, 11, 37, 82, 98, *108–117,* 122, 123
Watch That Ends the Night, The, 2, 11, 29–30, 40, 47, 51, 54, 55, 77, *82–93,* 94, 98, 102–103, 105, 106, 107, 110, 114, 119, 120, 123, 126

WORKS: NONFICTION:
"Are We a Godless People?" 92
"Changing Values in Fiction," 81
Cross-Country, 92
"Homage to Hemingway," 80–81
Oxyrhynchus: An Economic and Social Study, 23–24, 117
"Reflections on Two Decades," 97, 99, 101
Rivers of Canada, 107
"Roman History and To-Day," 24–26
Scotchman's Return and Other Essays, 79
Seven Rivers of Canada, 107
Thirty and Three, 79

MacLennan, Samuel, 3–6, 7, 11, 66, 70–72, 119; *see also* MacLennan, Hugh, relationship with his father
Mailer, Norman: *The Naked and the Dead,* 81
Matrist. *See* Taylor, Gordon Rattray
Mitchell, W. O., 1, 118
Montreal, Quebec, 9–11, 107–108
Montrealer, 11, 79, 124
More, Paul Elmer, 125
Morris, Desmond, 107
Munro, Alice, 119

New humanism, 125–26
Nock, Albert Jay: *Memoirs of a Superfluous Man,* 126–27, 134n16

Orwell, George: *Nineteen Eighty-Four,* 117

Oxford University, England, 7–8, 9, 124

Paton, Alan: *Cry, the Beloved Country*, 81
Patrist. *See* Taylor, Gordon Rattray
Penfield, Wilder, 126
Princeton University, New Jersey, 8–9, 20, 110, 125

Rabinovitch, Reuben, 87
Rohmer, Richard, 119
Ross, Sinclair, 1, 118, 119

Saturday Night, 11, 79
Scott, Walter, 32
Service, Robert, 31
Shakespeare: *King Lear*, 19
Stead, Robert, 31

Student Protest, 94, 95, 97

Tallman, Warren: "Wolf in the Snow," 76
Taylor, Gordon Rattray: *Sex in History*, 96–98, 99, 109
Tolstoy, Leo, 42, 122

Wasserman, Jakob: *The World's Illusion*, 42
Waugh, Evelyn, 81
Wilson, Edmund, 97, 127
Wilson, Ethel, 118, 119
Woodcock, George, 118, 127; "A Nation's Odyssey," 120
World War I, 3, 4–5, 32, 70, 82, 110, 114, 125
World War II, 14–15, 32, 38, 52, 78, 82, 111–12, 115, 125